*Being deeply loved by someone gives you strength,
While loving someone deeply gives you courage.*

Lao Tzu

I'LL BUY YOU
HEAVEN

Merle A. Miller

First published in 2024 by Hansib Publications
76 High Street, Hertford, SG14 3TA, United Kingdom

info@hansibpublications.com
www.hansibpublications.com

Copyright © Merle A. Miller, 2024

Merle A. Miller has asserted her right to be identified as the author of this work in accordance with the Copyright, Designs and Patents Act 1988.

Front cover photograph by Tazra Miller
Cover design concept by The Vellum Group, LLC

ISBN 978-1-0686993-3-7

A CIP catalogue record for this book is available from the British Library

All rights reserved. No part of this publication may be reproduced, stored in a retrieval system, or transmitted, in any form or by any means, electronic, mechanical, photocopying, recording or otherwise, without the prior permission of the author.

Produced and printed in Great Britain

Founded in London in 1970, Hansib Publications has played a crucial role in documenting the Caribbean experience and bringing Caribbean perspectives to a wider audience. It is renowned for its extensive catalogue of Caribbean fiction and non-fiction, spanning a diverse range of genres, including historical novels, biographies, poetry anthologies, political commentaries and social narratives. It has also made significant contributions to Caribbean scholarship by publishing insightful works on history, culture, politics and social issues.

Today, Hansib Publications remains a significant force in the world of Caribbean publishing and continues to publish books that reflect the vibrant diversity of the Caribbean region and the global Caribbean diaspora. Its legacy of promoting Caribbean voices and perspectives has made it an invaluable resource for those seeking to understand and appreciate the rich cultural heritage of the Caribbean.

To my grandchildren,

Leo, Jasper, Lily and Ruby – for all the joy you brought your Grandy and the joy you continue to bring me.

And in memory of you, my beloved and noble oak. You loved well!

PROLOGUE

Today

My dear, dear Brey,

Now our grandchildren will know of our life together. Hope you don't mind me sharing some of your letters with them. Brey, you would be so proud of how they are growing into thoughtful and caring people. Their parents are doing a great job.

I told them they will not be reading this book until they are at least eighteen years old. The boys accepted my decision, the girls fretted, "Why not Grammie, we're old enough now?" One day Brey, we will know of their greatness and how they embraced life with zest, pride, and dignity. And our hearts will smile!

Incidentally, every letter to you since your passing, with the exception of this one, was written in the mornings between 3 am and 6 am. Always the saddest time of day for me. I don't know why I'm telling you this, perhaps and hopefully, you were with me at that time of day.

I laughed, cried, pondered and emptied my heart into this book. And yet I feel there is so much more to tell, especially to our daughters.

Tazra and I were having a conversation about life, death, and everything in between, when she asked what intangible legacy I would like to pass on to her and Aliya.

Without hesitating I told her, "Search your soul, then listen to your intuition, never waver and it will never fail you."

As for me, I am thankful for both phases of my life. The past has been most intriguing, and incredibly happy. I am now content to harness my sorrow, and never think of what might have been, but soar in life's beauty with the knowledge that my happiness does not depend on circumstances, only on myself.

God must be within me, for I can again appreciate His glory at the break of dawn; always on the faces of children; and I am forever awed by the order of nature.

My darling, I am also at peace with my solitude. I count the stars again; notice how high the birds fly; lose myself in a book, with a cup of Darjeeling; play my music loudly – it calms my soul – and listen to the wind as if God is speaking to me. But most of all, Brey, He makes me aware of the love I'm still capable of, in both giving and receiving. That's how I know I'm graced with His presence. And I thank Him again and again!

Dear Brey, my present life is so much more bearable because of my past. I feel privileged for all the memories so clearly etched in my mind.

Sharing forty-seven years with you has increased my – still limited – wisdom about life and the challenges of living it. Also, these sunset moments have their advantages. Many days I sit quietly with my cup of tea, reminiscing on the times when my heart did beat faster, and my soul trembled as I walked on air. All for you, and because of you!

I am content for now. My life has not come full circle. Not yet! Only when we are together again. Wishful thinking? I hope not!

My love always and beyond,
Merle

The ancient Masters slept without dreams and woke up without worries.

Their food was plain. Their breath came from deep inside them.

They didn't cling to life, and weren't anxious about death.

They emerged without desire and re-entered without resistance.

They came easily; they went easily.

They didn't forget where they came from; they didn't ask where they were going.

They took everything as it came, gladly, and walked into death without fear.

They accepted life as a gift, and they handed it back gratefully.

Chuang Tzu

ONE

A horrible twist of fate and Aubrey's life is over. How could I have prevented it, held onto him, protected him? I must not weep anymore, tears are counterproductive. I repeatedly tell myself, "As of tomorrow, no more crying." But today is already 'tomorrow' and I can't seem to contain the tears! I have to think, convince my heart to be brave and not go to that place inside my head where only confusion reigns. Focus on surviving without my soulmate.

My thoughts are interrupted by the voices of our grandchildren playing in the backyard. I walked to our bedroom window and watched them frolicking in the snow, climbing the playhouse and swinging on the rope, all with such unlimited energy and exuberance. Aubrey and I used to call out to them from this very window, they would then put on an acrobatic show for us, each trying to outdo the other. I now listen to their laughter, forever the sweetest sound, even when my heart seems to have gone astray. As I tap on the window, they look up and for a second I think they expected to see their Grandy standing next to me. Then the moment passed. Whatever the season, our grands always enjoy the backyard, along with the rabbits, squirrels, birds and the occasional deer darting between the trees.

My eyes divert to the landscape. Such tall pine trees, their snow-covered tips giving them a majestic look, like white crowns on green giants. A ravine flows between our backyard and a conservation park that has many tall birch trees. On windy mornings between spring and fall, one can hear the rustling of the branches, their leaves flirting with the clouds, and the soothing sound of the mourning doves call. Nature's alarm to awaken you, feeling elated without a cause. That's how I felt waking up beside Aubrey. When will I adjust to living without him? Speak of him in the past tense? And when will I find myself again, my whole self, one person instead of half of a couple? There must be a positive side to this lost lonely feeling. But when and how? Seeking God helps sometimes. I have to exercise more faith for my sanity and comfort.

As I watch my grandchildren's antics, I think of how as children we are imaginative, uninhibited, happy and live in the moment. Then as adults, we are burdened by fear, greed, hurt and many other emotional turmoils. So much to bear, the self is lost. We then become wandering souls in this vast jungle, worrying about tomorrow, regretting yesterday, while forgetting how to live today. I pray my grandchildren always remember to live in the moment.

I went downstairs as the boisterous four came in, snow-covered, hungry and hoping to be entertained by Grammie. I provided snacks and a deck of playing cards. Then with full stomachs, tired limbs, bold statements and endless questions, which include Leo's "Guess what? Grammie never saw snow until she was very, very old!" (22 years). Jasper remembered his Grandy teaching him how to play poker. Then Lily asked, "Grammie, how was your life in Guyana and when did you and Grandy meet and fall in love?" The eldest, (Leo) in his best authoritative voice said, "Lily, don't ask Grammie such personal questions!" And our youngest, Ruby, who spent a few formative years in her Grandy's company, as he taught her so much – including, introducing her to the moon – claimed sadly, "I miss Grandy; he always helped me with my jigsaw puzzles."

As I listen to their questions and declarations, I think now is the time to enlighten our munchkins about my 'snowless' life in Guyana, and the years their Grandy and I shared. For, I believe, some moments in life are too splendid to be contained. Our grandchildren should know!

TWO

Guyana is the only English-speaking country in South America, and although it is part of that vast continent, it is culturally Caribbean. Prior to nearly four centuries of European colonisation, Guyana was only inhabited by indigenous Amerindian communities.

The Dutch were the first Europeans to establish colonies and they ruled from the late 1500s until the British assumed control towards the end of the 18th century. The colonies were formally ceded to Britain in 1814, and in 1831 they were united into what became the single colony of British Guiana. In 1966, my country achieved independence from Britain and was renamed Guyana.

Guyana – which is divided into three counties, Berbice, Essequibo, and Demerara where the capital Georgetown is located – is approximately 215.000 square kilometres (slightly smaller than the United Kingdom) with a population of around 800,000, the majority of whom are primarily the descendants of enslaved peoples brought from Africa and indentured labourers from India during the era of colonial rule. The multiracial population also included the various Indigenous Amerindian communities and those of Chinese and European heritage.

Although Guyanese people socialised and worked together happily and peacefully, marriage outside of one's own race was strongly discouraged.

With each cultural group came a wealth of traditions, customs and also cuisines. Over many years, the various food influences across the cultures, plus the inclusion of local herbs and spices, evolved into a flavour that was uniquely 'Guyanese'.

This land of my birth also produces gold, diamonds, bauxite, rice and the famed 'Demerara' sugar. The name 'Guyana' is an Indigenous word that means 'land of many waters' – a reflection of the country's many rivers, tributaries, waterfalls, lakes and the forceful Atlantic Ocean to the north. Much of the land's beauty lies in the interior, particularly within the rainforests which are abundant with flora and fauna. The most impressive, in my opinion, are the birds, of which there are over seven hundred species. Many parrots or macaws were kept as pets, and being in a domestic environment, some spoke quite fluently.

A most amusing incident I recall. During the 1967 Expo in Montreal, Guyana sent a colourful macaw to enhance their pavilion. To acclimatise, the bird arrived early and was there while the pavilion was being built. During the construction, Macaw Millie was around the workers so much that she became fluent in French, acquiring some explicit, undesirable adjectives. Unfortunately, because of her extensive vocabulary in both English and French, Millie had to be sent home prior to the official opening. Despite missing the event, she arrived home a bilingual celebrity, and was eventually acknowledged on a postage stamp.

The Essequibo river is the longest in Guyana and has many inhabited islands. Leguan, the place of my birth, is one of the islands on this river. Just fourteen kilometres long and approximately three kilometres wide, Leguan has an abundance of fruit trees, rice fields and beautiful sandy beaches. I don't recall living there, as my parents moved to Georgetown when I was very young. However, the little island played a major role during my childhood. Our summer holidays were spent there with my relatives and friends, beachcombing and having fun all day, returning to Georgetown just in time for uniform fittings and school.

To get to Leguan from the capital, you had to take a ferry across the Demerara river, then a train to Parika – a small village, on the west coast of Demerara – and finally, another ferry on the Essequibo river to the island. Parika had many fruit vendors and before boarding the second ferry, we always bought bananas. The train ride and 'Parika bananas' were the highlights of my journey. Those small bananas, with an almost translucent peel, were available only at the Parika train station. I have never seen them anywhere else in Guyana; the only other place was in Thailand, many years later.

Some say memories during one's childhood remain with them throughout their lives. Trivial events or not, the mind selects and retains pinnacle childhood moments.

One summer, my two sisters, a cousin, and I were on our annual trip to Leguan. We each carried a piece of luggage and being the youngest, I was given the smallest and lightest one. After the long train ride, we departed at Parika. With my eyes focused on the banana vendors, all the while trying to keep up with the others, I marched with purpose, my free arm swinging nonchalantly. Unknown to me, the clasp on my suitcase gave away and the contents fell out. I just kept on walking towards my favourite bananas, almost tasting their delicious flavour, while oblivious to the swinging empty suitcase. Meanwhile, walking behind me were two gentlemen retrieving all the contents from my grip.

My older sister and cousin were embarrassed and also terribly angry with me. Needless to say, we went directly onto the ferry. I later watched as the banana vendors grew smaller and smaller as we sailed away, while feeling terribly disappointed. Also, I didn't understand why my sister was making such a fuss over our underwear. It was not like they were lost, the kind gentlemen collected and returned them all. Regardless, no bananas that trip!

Throughout my childhood, I believed Leguan was *our* island. What prompted that arrogant assumption? My maternal grandmother owned acres of rice fields, parcels of land, cattle, fruit and vegetable farms. Some of our ancestral land is, to this day, still in the family. Both she and my grandfather were from India.

My grandfather came to Guyana as a merchant and had a textile business in Georgetown. He married my grandmother, a widow with five children. They then had four more children together. Their wedding must have been an elaborate event as we have a copy of the occasion, which was published in the newspapers.

Dada and Nanee (paternal grandparents) also lived in Essequibo County, but on the coast. Dada arrived from India as an indentured labourer. Nanee was the only Guyanese born of my four grandparents. They had ten children, which included four sons, with my father being the only surviving son. Nanee was also the only grandparent I knew, the others passed away prior to my birth.

After Dada died, she spent her remaining years living among her children. Although a haughty and feisty lady who was not always endearing, everything about my grandmother fascinated me, including her wardrobe. Nanee's attire was ankle-length skirts and long-sleeved blouses. Under her skirt was what she referred to as her petticoat and under her blouse, a shimmy. Her long grey hair was braided, then rolled in a bun and covered with a scarf, which was always white.

On her wrists she wore thick silver bangles and each ear was adorned with gold rings; one ear with seven, the other eight. There is a reason for the tradition of uneven earrings, she explained it all to me once, I presume this information was not interesting enough for a young person to retain.

I never saw Nanee with a purse. Her money was always in a drawstring cloth pouch which was hung from her waist and when she went out, the pouch was concealed between her skirt and petticoat.

We truly bonded when she visited us, I think some of my precocious ways surprised and amused her. She, in turn, intrigued me; her arrogance and strange mannerisms never phased me. I used to sit on her bed bombarding her with questions about her life. One evening, while scrutinising her rings, I asked her if the ornate one was her engagement ring.

Nanee had no idea what 'engagement' meant. She was then given the full explanation from her very young granddaughter.

She and Dada worked hard and accumulated rice fields, a coconut estate, fishing boats, a rice mill, a general store and other businesses. However, the wealth from both maternal and paternal grandparents did not filter down to the grandchildren; it must have been badly managed by the previous generation.

THREE

When I was seven years old, I was hospitalised for reasons still unknown to me. I remember Ma rocking me, her lovely scent, her warmth and soothing voice.

As a little girl, I had mixed emotions about being in the hospital, and I missed my parents terribly. On the other hand, I had daily visits and received beautiful gifts, such as a lovely and highly impractical pair of beaded slippers that Ma had previously denied me, after I spied them in a shop window. I also had my two beloved story books with me. The only inconvenience seemed to be the daily injections administered and the chore of having to eat. All that I was told years later regarding my time spent in the hospital, was being allergic to penicillin and having a rare blood type.

Every morning while hospitalised, my brother Kash, twelve years my senior, brought me my favourite comic strips, 'Mutt & Jeff' 'Maggie & Jiggs' and 'Blondie', neatly cut from the daily newspapers. Kash also brought small wooden toys he made in his spare time to keep me entertained. He was a gifted woodworker and made my sister and I beautiful dolls' furniture, so intricately done, we thought it was the work of Santa's elves.

I'm sure I had frequent visits from my other siblings, especially Arif, the third eldest of my brothers, who affectionately called me "Bones," a monicker he still uses today. Arif, my jovial and charismatic brother, always had time to take my sister Zorena and I driving and sometimes organised trips to the beach with us and our friends. He knew how we hated taking our daily dose of cod liver oil and would reward whoever reminded him to administer it. Zorena, whom I presume didn't mind the taste, became quite rich, while I had to continue taking the ghastly oil and was poorer for it.

Niz, the fourth of my brothers, was and still is the most mischievous. He derived much pleasure in teasing his younger sisters and always tried to shift his naughty pranks on us.

Zorena, three years my senior, and I are close, we did everything together as kids. I remember as teenagers how she always looked out for me, especially when we attended parties. I don't know if it was her protective instinct or the responsibility imposed by our parents. It must have been tiring to take care of another when you yourself were so young. She was level-headed and responsible; I in turn, the opposite.

The eldest of my brothers, Zed, sixteen years my senior was like another parent to me. One who also indulged my every whim. Sometimes, while he was courting my sister-in-law, Lyla, who lived outside of the city, I was taken along to visit; I'm sure at my insistence. She came from a family with no small children and, therefore, I was showered with attention. I recall my naps after our Sunday lunches with them. My siesta room had many little trinkets which I loved playing with when they thought I was having a much-needed rest.

Khalda, my eldest sister, and her husband Hassan are the ones responsible for getting me hooked on Second World War movies; a period in history that still interests me. I remember being a pre-teen munching through mouthfuls of Smarties, my eyes glued to the screen, as I rooted for the good guys.

I spent many happy years with my siblings, and being the youngest in a family of seven was indeed advantageous. Now, reflecting on the relationship I have with them, I see they each influenced my life in a different and positive way. The common bond was their love and caring attitude. I hope they are aware that this feeling is reciprocated.

FOUR

Our home was the meeting place. Relatives and friends were in and out constantly. Family gatherings were boisterous and happy. I am blessed with many aunts, uncles and cousins. Also, friends of Ma, Pa and my adult siblings were always around.

Ma, an accomplished cook, derived much pleasure in feeding everyone. She spoilt us with fun foods and all our guests were treated to a meal or some sort of delicious treat. Like most children, I had little interest in eating, for it infringed on my playtime. I recall being fed, and I am too embarrassed to divulge my age when this ridiculous overindulgence took place.

My mother was a huge influence in my life. There is so much I have learnt by just growing up around her. Ma taught me to be kind through her deeds and actions. I recall as a child, my girlfriend and I had some sort of disagreement and she complained to her mother, who then told Ma. I was promptly summoned to our dining room table where Ma said, "So you were not nice to Tessa. I just want to say, whenever you think of being unkind to anyone, first ask yourself, 'Would I like the same done to me?' If the answer is 'yes', then go right ahead and do it." She got up and left me sitting there with my thoughts. I was never given the opportunity to state my case, much less defend it. At that tender age, I learnt a valuable lesson and hope I still practice what Ma taught me.

I remember her constantly telling me to be respectful to adults by not asking any questions. I used to observe most people, totally intrigued, be they friends of my parents, relatives, or just acquaintances. Regardless of the relationship, I always had a question that needed clarifying, which, according to Ma, was rude or inappropriate. My dear mother was forever horrified! Her stern warning to me when we were around anyone was, "No questions, or else!" I never knew what 'else' meant, it just had a negative connotation which was enough to curb my inquisitive mind.

Ma was also the one who instilled values and a code of ethics in us. At her insistence, everyone who ever worked in our home was treated with respect and kindness and they were never taken for granted; especially Mother Warner, whom we considered a member of our family. My mother always used stories from "Aesop's Fables" and "The Royal Reader" as examples of how to behave and treat others. I have never read either of the books. "The Royal Reader" must have been her book as a schoolgirl, but I knew the stories through her.

All of Ma's efforts of fostering in us a sense of kindness began or ended with a story. She seemed to have a tale for everything. How I loved when my mother sang to me. 'Little Waves' was one of the songs my siblings and I especially enjoyed. When my girls and I were in England, Arif sometimes sang to them. One morning, Aliya ran to me confused and a little amazed, "Mom, Uncle Arif is singing our song." I then realised my brother had passed on the tradition of singing 'Little Waves' to his children. I also sang it to my grandchildren. I am not familiar with who wrote the lyrics or the original singer. Ma was the only person who performed for us. No wonder we adopted it as our lullaby. Maybe someday our grandchildren will sing it to their children.

My father devoted a lot of time to his children as well, and though strict, he sometimes indulged us. Pa had a particular style of solving our conflicts and curiosity. One day, after having had enough of Zorena and I arguing, he said whenever one complained about the other, he would punish us both. We quickly learned to get along. Another time he caught me trying to smoke a piece of rolled-up paper, nearly setting our bathroom on fire. He told my eldest brother who smoked, to teach me how, and Zed proceeded to do so. We sat at our dining room table. This was a place where all our debates, laughter and teasing – especially during our Sunday breakfasts that lasted hours – took place, and now my smoking lesson. I coughed and gagged, but didn't give up. That day I learnt to inhale the smoke, swallow a mouthful of water, and then exhale. Quite a feat! I was rather proud of my achievement. I knew Pa was observing, while pretending to be going about his business. His tactic worked, for after smoking that one cigarette I'd had my fill. With my interest satisfied, my smoking habit started and ended that day. I was about eleven or twelve years old and have not smoked since.

Pa was also handy and creative; he always helped with projects such as toy building, kite making, and even invaded the kitchen sometimes to make us delicious taffy, which we referred to as 'stretcher.' According to Pa, pulling the candy made it more chewable. When I was a Girl Guide Cadet and had to build a small tent, my father happily helped me until late into the evening. I also remember the jigsaw puzzle board he made, with a raised border, making it more convenient to move my puzzle to any part of our home.

During the sixties, Pa lived part-time in the Rupununi District where he planted tobacco. He occupied a villa there and flew back and forth to Georgetown. At that time there were few commercial flights to the savannah, so everyone travelled by 'cattle plane.' Most of Guyana's cattle was reared in Rupununi and little propeller planes flew the slaughtered meat to the capital.

When I was seventeen, I spent a week during the Easter holidays with him. It was on this trip that I missed the opportunity of eating iguana meat. We went over the border to Brazil and were invited by a warm and hospitable Amerindian family to partake in their meal. I watched as they scraped the green pigment off by pouring hot water over it. Once the meat was cut up it looked similar to chicken breast. I remember thinking, "Why not, I'm game and I think iguanas are safe to eat, as they are herbivores." I also assumed it was impolite to refuse. However, my father did not share my appetite for open-fired lizard and he graciously refused on behalf of both of us.

I was in Rupununi during its annual rodeo and there was always some form of entertainment going on. One morning in our eagerness to arrive on time for an event, my friend and I were running and I fell, cutting my leg badly. Due to the heat and the running, it bled profusely. Meti, the Amerindian lady who took care of my father's villa, immediately took charge of the situation. She went out to Pa's (not too well manicured) garden and carefully collected some leaves. She crushed the leaves, then started to rub them together between the palms of her hands, moisturising it with her saliva. Meti then covered my wound with the poultice and Pa bandaged it. After approximately three hours, my cut lost its redness and in forty-eight hours was completely healed. I was too young and carefree – also elated that my wound did not infringe on my remaining days of fun – to inquire about what leaves Meti used, and Pa was busy attending his tobacco plants. He never asked her about those miraculous healing plants. I believe the indigenous people of South America were never given much opportunity to teach us their knowledge and wisdom. Regretfully, I think we are still missing out!

Most evenings after supper, when I wasn't hanging out with the cattle baron's teens – whom I befriended from school in the city – Pa and I would each occupy a hammock, swinging under the stars. His workers were Amerindians and he told some amusing and heart-warming stories about them and their unique and amazing culture.

After a day in the hot sun attending the annual rodeo, I looked forward to my father's tales; he was so good at telling them. As little girls, Zorena and I used to sit on his lap, totally engrossed as he entertained us. The look on his face always indicated he was about to tell us the most interesting and exciting stories. I'm sure those tales were made up as he went along, but were nevertheless enjoyable. They were accompanied with funny or scary facial expressions, depending on what was required. Pa did the same with his grandchildren; they still talk about their grandfather's famous tales and claim no one embellished a story quite like their Papa! He was also an amateur magician and I enjoyed all the tricks with which he entertained us. Pa was indeed a fun father. No wonder our friends, who still address my parents as "Ma and Pa", enjoyed coming over to our home. Ma supplied the goodies and Pa the entertainment.

Years later when they objected to Aubrey and I marrying, I thought of all the love, comfort and wisdom I received from my parents. Throughout my years, they befriended, embraced, and entertained friends of different ethnicities and religions in our home. At the time I wondered, "Why were they being so difficult now?"

FIVE

Like most children, Christmas was my favourite time of year. During the season, families went window shopping after dinner. Zorena and I loved a particular shop window display. It involved a fan, balloons and bright coloured ribbon. When the fan was on, the balloons which were contained by the ribbons danced in the air. It was simple, creative and unique. We were dazzled. In fact, we were so enthralled, that a few days later Pa recreated one in our home.

After looking at all the shop windows with much wishful longing, we were treated to ice cream cones and then home to bed. On such outings so close to Christmas, sleep always evaded me. One year, while window shopping, I saw a walking doll wearing a green velvet dress. Praying and being a well-behaved little girl didn't work that Christmas; she did not appear under our tree. During one of our reminiscent conversations, I told Aubrey about the doll I never got. He related a similar story about wanting a six-shooter gun with a rotating barrel. Back then cowboys and Indians were the main form of play for most little boys. With his face against the shop window, eyes focused on the gun, and saying every prayer to God and the Saints – being a Catholic, I believe that was the order of prayers – Father Christmas brought him a regular capped gun and not the one of his dreams.

I don't think Aubrey and I were the exception. Most children in the fifties received few presents. The United Kingdom was just recovering from the Second World War and being a British colony we were also affected.

A visit to Father Christmas was a special day in town. To visit the jolly man, sit on his lap and receive a toy, cost our parents a shilling (twenty-four cents), fifty-cents, or a dollar. Of course, the quality of your gift depended on the price of your ticket. As children we weren't aware of such unnecessary information, whatever present we received made us happy. After Santa, we went on to 'Brown Betty' for lunch, where my order was always a strawberry ice cream soda and a cheese sandwich cut in triangles, with no crust.

On Christmas Eve we slept in new pyjamas and prior to settling in for the night, we placed a pillowcase at the foot of our bed. In it, Father Christmas left us sweeties, balloons, nuts and, for some lucky kids, an ice apple. Apples and grapes were imported and available only during the festive season. Because of the climate they were packed in cool containers for shipping, hence the term, 'ice apples'. Getting an apple in your pillowcase was indeed a treat. I never got one and always had to settle for slices distributed by someone older. The toys Father Christmas left under our tree were never gift wrapped or labelled. Zorena and I knew they were for us and we shared. I passed on the same tradition of unwrapped toys from Santa to Aliya and Tazra. Decorating the house and tree was a Christmas Eve tradition, accompanied by the delicious aroma coming from the kitchen, while listening to the seasonal music provided by our only radio station, 'Radio Demerara'; all amidst the confusion and excitement of friends or relatives dropping in to exchange greetings.

The season was always the time to renovate and upgrade your home. Even to date, certain smells like new linoleum – which was our annual kitchen floor refurbishing – or wooden floor polish, still reminds me of the Christmases of yesteryear.

After a wonderful childhood, came my teenage years which were restricted by my parents, especially Pa. With Ma I could persuade her with pleading and hugs; whereas with Pa, one did not plead or bribe, you had to simply ask. Timing was the trick. I learnt to recognise his moods and when not to approach him concerning the most important events in my life, such as

Aubrey 12 or 13 years old. I was not a happy five-year-old flower girl.

attending a party, or any social gathering not chaperoned by parents, siblings, or the occasional cousin. Pa rarely gave in, and sometimes kept Zorena or I waiting for over a week before saying firmly "Merly, you're not going!" with no reason to justify his decision. Those were trying times, for not being able to attend a party was incredibly stressful. On the rare occasion, when the hurdle of obtaining permission was granted, I then had to negotiate my return time.

One evening, Zorena and I were not happy with our curfew, so we turned the clock back an hour prior to leaving the house, this took a bit of nerve but as the saying goes, "Desperate times call for desperate measures". I was on the lookout while Zorena adjusted the time. The tricky part was readjusting it upon returning from the party. Pa always waited up for us, and on that particular evening he was still up long after we returned and were in bed. After hours of dancing, it was especially difficult to stay awake while waiting for him to settle in, so we could sneak back into the living room and adjust the time.

A festival took place in October 1961 with various steel bands competing and portraying historical and mythical characters.

Each band consisted of over a hundred members, all in colourful costume; not unlike a carnival but on a smaller scale. Since Guyana's independence, this festival has been replaced with 'Mashramani', an Indigenous word meaning 'celebration of hard work', which now occurs annually in February. With some persuasion from Zorena and I, our parents agreed for me to participate in the 1961 festival. Zorena was not interested in joining. This was just as well, for she took on the task of looking out for me, I'm sure at my parents' insistence. The band I joined was 'Helen of Troy'.

Little did I know, amidst the excitement and confusion, I would meet a young man who would delight and bewilder me, while I was being enlightened to the ways of the heart.

My life was changed forever!

SIX

"There is nothing holier in this life of ours than the first consciousness of love – the first fluttering of its silken wings – the first rising sound and breath of that wind which is so soon to sweep through the soul, to purify or destroy."

Henry Wadsworth Longfellow

The Gods smiled down on me the day I was introduced to Aubrey Miller. I met him at the home of Shirley and Godfrey Chin. Godfrey was the chief organiser of 'Helen of Troy' and all the costume preparation was done in their home.

Meeting Aubrey was no heart-pounding experience, just a casual introduction to a handsome guy with impeccable manners and a good sense of humour. His 'impeccable manners' did not go unnoticed by Shirley. She told me that during many a late night, when some of the guys and girls were busy making costumes, she served them coffee. Aubrey never failed to thank her and comment on how delicious it tasted. Shirley knew otherwise, but appreciated his complement.

For approximately six months prior to the festival, their home was bombarded with characters from Homer's *The Iliad*: Hector, Ajax, Helen, Paris, Achilles, Menelaus, slaves, Amazons and many others. Some folks were very involved and worked late into the evenings for months, while maintaining full-time jobs. They were busy researching at the library, buying materials, sheets of copper, cork and other necessities to sew or embellish costumes. Apart from making their own, they

Aubrey in full regalia

were also helping others. I recall Aubrey working on my sandals and during one of the fittings, after measuring, re-measuring and cutting the straps, in a frustrated and accusing tone, he claimed, "Your feet are too small for an Amazon's." Somehow, I felt I should have apologised for having small feet. Most of our conversation was related to my costume, we hardly spoke otherwise; especially after his comment about my feet. Many times it was just a smile or nod of acknowledgement and strangely, the less he said, the more intrigued I was about him.

One day the Amazons had to get wigs and hats fitted. This took place at the home of Aubrey's friend. Mike's home was large enough to accommodate us all. His mother was out of the country, which, I believe was what prompted Mike to open his home to us girls. When we arrived, there were more Greek and Trojan warriors than Amazons; of course this led to a lot of flirting and teasing during costume fittings.

When my sister and I were ready to leave, I couldn't find my shoes. Unknown to me, Aubrey had hidden them with the hope I would stay a little longer. He must have been quite observant when we arrived, as there were at least a dozen pairs of black shoes all together. He told me years later that he had arranged with Paulus, another friend of his, to render his services of pretending to look for them, giving Aubrey time to get better acquainted with me. He was determined to keep me there a while longer.

That was when I realised Aubrey Miller was attracted to me. The feeling must have been mutual, for my heart skipped a beat. I don't recall much but what I do remember was riding on a cloud all the way home. Zorena and I arrived later than expected and needless to say, Pa fretted. That particular evening I wasn't bothered, solely because my heart was still in the clouds!

I looked forward to costume fittings only because Aubrey was there. We shared many interests; the movies, reading, history and the upcoming festival. Our friendship developed and by the night our band was appearing on stage to be judged, I knew our relationship was beyond platonic. A fitting description by Ann Landers is, "Love is friendship that has caught fire". And I believe it has no regard for time or age, for as a mere teenager I fell in love with my friend and that passion lasted for over half a century.

Everyone danced in the streets, or on floats, to the music of steel bands. The floats were authentic and colourful; ours included a huge wooden horse. Four of us were on that float; two Greek soldiers – one of them was Aubrey's brother, Richard – another Amazon and myself. After the parade, the bands assembled at a huge park to be judged. 'Helen of Troy' placed second, thanks to Godfrey and all the skilled men and women involved.

Afterwards, our sponsor threw us a celebration party at a popular nightclub which was reserved exclusively for us that evening. Pa refused to let me attend. Some of my girlfriends pleaded on my behalf, but he didn't give in. I cried myself to sleep that night.

The following day I heard of the many toasts from friends. Aubrey's glass was never empty. He vaguely remembered that party, I can well imagine why.

SEVEN

Having a steady boyfriend and dating was taboo, for my parents would never have sanctioned such a lifestyle. Moreover, being of East Indian descent, they would not have accepted my dating a man of a different ethnicity. However, by then I had developed a daring and defiant attitude. I was ecstatic and totally smitten with Aubrey.

The young men I knew seemed juvenile compared to him, but then he was four years older than I. He had a quiet, mature way and was always tolerant with my sometimes silly outbursts of whatever I said without thought. We met secretly and rarely, with the festival being over I had no reason to be out in the evenings. Aubrey exercised a lot of patience and understanding, especially when I had to break our dates at the last minute with no logical explanation other than, "I can't get away." By then I was running out of believable excuses to keep my rendezvous with him. That was where the guilt came in. My parents believed whatever I told them until someone saw us together at the movies and it was reported back to them. A lady whom I never knew, told my sister-in-law. Lyla, then told my brother Zed, who passed on this information to Ma and Pa. The saying, "It takes a village to raise a child", is a way of life in our country. Every relative, friend, neighbour, or domestic help, felt it was their duty to oversee your upbringing.

Pa and Ma forbade me from seeing Aubrey. They had met him only once, when he visited us, and they thought him to be a casual friend. However, now he was just another young man who was not welcomed in my life. Pa was very angry, and Ma lectured me of the consequences and the lengths they would go to prevent me from meeting him. I then realised this was not about me, only my parents, their friends, our relatives and what the rest of their little world would think. After all, 'well brought up' Indo-Guyanese daughters were denied the pleasure of dating. This was a new experience for them and me, and feeling a little scared and intimidated, I promised not to continue my friendship with Aubrey and I meant it. The constant worry of being seen together, along with the attraction I felt for him left me excited, confused and wary. I was not experienced or mature enough to deal with a situation that was becoming increasingly stressful. At first, Aubrey accepted my decision. However, after a couple months of unsuccessful attempts to reach me, he showed up at one of our Cub meetings – I was one of three Cub leaders – and refused to leave until I agreed to go to the movies with him. Of course, I relented!

Between our secret dates, we led separate social lives. I went to a few parties with parent approved folks and Aubrey socialised with his circle of friends, whom I didn't know. We had some friends in common and when possible we got together. The irony of it all was that my parents did not need to worry, for our dates were innocent ... well, mostly.

Many years later, Aubrey teased me about what he referred to as my "famous line." When I felt our emotions could get out of control, the vision of Pa was like a splash of cold water on my face and the line he referred to was, "Brey, remove your hand!" He respected my wishes and exercised a lot of patience and tolerance, especially when I always had to leave any event early, regardless of how good a time we were having. How I loved those days, even with the restrictions enforced by my parents, which was to be home before dark, unless I went to the cinema.

The movies allowed us a couple more hours. Ma thought I went with whomever I mentioned; all the approved names were used. I now cringe when I think of how they trusted me,

Affiance, Essequibo, left, and Red Water Creek, Demerara

especially after promising not to meet Aubrey again! Going to the movies provided our only bit of privacy. Always back row in balcony, second and third seats from the window. We knew each cinema's layout and the seats we preferred. Strangely, those seats were never occupied. We arrived and left separately; Aubrey always came in after the movie started, dark enough so he would not be noticed, or more so, that I wouldn't be recognised when he sat down next to me. He left before the ending, waiting for me around the corner. We rode up to a few houses before mine, then parted ways.

During our stolen moments in the park or his home we discussed everything, including books we'd read. Apart from historical books, I also enjoyed Agatha Christie and Mickey

Spillane novels, which he bought me regardless of my protests. Most of them I had already read, but didn't have the heart to say so. Many months later, I eventually donated them to the Georgetown library. We also shared many discussions, from Greek philosophers, to movies and historical events, all between teasing, necking and laughter. I was never bored in his company.

Making plans as to where and when to meet next was always challenging, and it took up a lot of time; Georgetown has few places safe from prying eyes. Sometimes we met at a girlfriend's home just to find a place to socialise, where her mother and siblings were always around. Another girlfriend Helga, who now resides in Brazil, visited me a couple of years after Aubrey passed away. One evening while reminiscing about our youthful days, I mentioned how Aubrey and I always found it difficult locating places to meet discreetly. Helga asked why we didn't go to the infamous "Sea Wall".

Because Guyana's coastline is below sea level, a wall approximately four hundred and fifty kilometres long was built to keep out the Atlantic Ocean. The Sea Wall was a popular hangout for leisurely moonlight walks while enjoying the cool ocean breeze, and somewhere for lovers to meet. Perhaps Aubrey thought it was too public a place, and would have put me at risk of being seen with him. Regardless of the reason, he never suggested it, and it never occurred to me.

Helga, being Aubrey's friend prior to my knowing him, also mentioned how she warned him against dating me. She had gone through a similar situation. Her mother did not approve of the young man she was in love with, and because of the pressure and constant rows, Helga broke off the relationship. She told Aubrey he was wasting his time, for my parents would never agree to me dating anyone. According to Helga, an unperturbed Aubrey said, "One day she will be mine. That's the girl I'm going to marry!" She then told him, "If her father doesn't kill you first!"

I refer to those four years of sneaking out to be with Aubrey as, "The Clock Years" because it seemed as if my brain and

Aubrey and his mother, Doreen, in Toronto, 1968

heart were constantly calculating, debating, reasoning and thinking of ways to beat the time and gain a few more minutes with him. How he made my heart beat faster. To be young and in love is indeed pure euphoria!

Aubrey introduced me to his parents and friends in December 1961. The Miller family were hosting a Boxing Day open house. He had told his mother about me but never mentioned my name, so when we met she didn't know which girl he was interested in, as there were quite a few of us. Then she saw the gold chain and locket I wore and recognised it. It was my first Christmas gift from Aubrey. I addressed her as 'Mrs Miller' for over a year, although in typical Indo-Guyanese tradition, women old enough to be your mother, were considered an honorary member of your family and were addressed as 'Ma', 'Mom' or 'Aunty' but never 'Mrs.' After a while I decided to call her 'Mater' which was eventually adopted by all of my relatives and friends. Incidentally, her name was Doreen.

    I always thought of Mater as a career woman in the right time but the wrong place. A talented seamstress, she taught herself to sew at fourteen. Had Mater been in a more developed country, her couturier skills would have been equal to any modern fashion house. Her little black book, filled with clients' measurements, including mine, was carefully guarded. All you had to do was show her a sketch or photograph of what you wanted and with her extraordinary skill, Mater then created a pattern and made your outfit. She had developed a successful business and would often work late into the night. During one of our tête-a-têtes, Mater told me many evenings when Aubrey came in late after hanging out with his friends and saw her still sewing, he would sit and keep her company. I believe that's when he acquired his sewing sense and an eye for well-made clothing.

    His father was 'Mr Miller' to all, including myself. Somehow I knew the Indian tradition would not have pleased or suited him. I referred to him as 'Mr Miller' even after Aubrey and I were married. When I met Mr Miller, I thought of him as a cold, austere man and a little aloof, but after a few visits to their home, he and I developed a cordial relationship. Then when Aubrey left for Canada, 'Old Man Miller' (as Aubrey referred to him) and I became quite close. We would sit, chat and exchange books. He never hesitated to tell me exactly what he thought about any and everything. I rather enjoyed his company and most times found his occasionally condescending attitude amusing. About a year after Aubrey and I were married, Mr Miller wrote to me and asked, "Don't you think it's time for you to start addressing me as Dad?" I gladly obliged.

EIGHT

After four years of clandestine dates, Aubrey was leaving the country to continue his education and pursue a career. Regretfully, up until the sixties, post-secondary education was not available in Guyana. Hence, most parents sent their children abroad to further their education with the hope of them eventually returning. By then, three of his siblings were in the United Kingdom and Aubrey, the fourth of six children, was leaving for Canada. He would be living with Raymond, his mother's youngest brother, and Carmen, his wife. Raymond was eight years Aubrey's senior and they were quite close; more friends than uncle and nephew.

Four of my siblings were also abroad; two in the United Kingdom, one in the United States and one in Canada. I was eleven years old when my first sibling left and I recall how my mother was devastated. In Guyana, all children, regardless of age, lived at home until they were married or left the country. Aubrey told me his mother was just as upset when his siblings left and when it was his time to leave, his dad asked him to defer his trip for one year, giving her time to adjust to having her children move so far from home. Thank God for mothers! Because of that delay we met and the one-year deferral lasted four years.

It was now his time to leave! I had conflicting emotions about his impending departure. We discussed marriage briefly, though I doubted it would materialise. Although I grew up in an unorthodox Muslim home, my parents never considered their children marrying out of our religion or ethnicity. It was an unspoken understanding, and Aubrey being a Roman Catholic of African, Scottish and Portuguese descent, would not be a welcome partner. The barrier was just too wide. Even though Ma and Pa were first generation Guyanese, some of the Indian traditions were still embedded in their way of life. Indo-Guyanese parents were, in most cases, very much involved in their children meeting the 'right' person, with the hope that a relationship would develop and eventually lead to marriage. They arranged the marriages of my eldest brother Zed and my sister Khalda, and we celebrated their weddings in traditional Indian style with over five hundred guests. Both siblings enjoyed long lives with their spouses until a few years beyond their golden anniversaries, when my brother and brother-in-law passed away in their late seventies.

Now Aubrey was leaving for Canada and it seemed that fate had played its hand. Apart from the heartache, which I hoped would subside with time, I wouldn't have to deal with the constant worry of deceiving Ma and Pa anymore. This separation should get him out of my heart and into my head, where I could think sensibly and logically. I even wondered if these feelings could be infatuation, along with the challenge of defying my parents. If so, with him being away, maybe we would eventually develop different interests and a new love. I just couldn't visualise marriage on the horizon! Such futile thoughts! For even as a young inexperienced girl, I knew my heart never adhered to reasoning. I derived no consolation with all the logical assumptions and rationale, and was totally miserable!

He departed and I didn't hear from him for a month! I remembered feeling lonely and far from happy, but I kept telling myself, "It's all for the best," while still hoping for a letter. I also thought, "This must be love, being apart is too painful."

Then a letter arrived!

* * * * *

November 22/1965

Hello Love,

I know you expected to hear from me earlier and these few lines will not compensate for the weeks and hours of waiting anxiously, fear not my love, I have not given you up, if and when, you will know. I will try to relate briefly what has happened since my arrival. I got a job on the 25th Oct. and gave it up today for a better one, so much for jobs. As regards my other affairs I am getting on better than expected, for instance, Carmen does my laundry all I have to do is help with dinner and assist with cleaning the house on weekends. I know you are thinking, "you have it good, yet you did not write". Love let me give you a few facts as to why you didn't hear from me earlier.

1. Job hunting
2. After I acquired my first job, I had to leave home at 7am to be in for 8. I quit at 5pm. Getting home at 5:45pm with just enough time to help with dinner, eat, shave, shower and jump into bed, ALONE!
3. Carmen was in hospital for 10 days; you could imagine how busy Ray and I were for that period.

And lastly, we used our spare time apartment hunting; we succeeded and will be moving on the 15th Dec. I am sure you'll love it here. Must close now with lots of love and kisses. I love and miss you terribly. Take care of yourself.

Yours truly,
Brey.

Ps. Don't ever forget or doubt my love.

That was the first of ninety-one letters from Aubrey over the course of our life together. I have only a few of my ninety-one replies. Years later, I told him I wanted to destroy mine because of all the mush I must have written. We kept our letters separately.

After he passed away, I found only a few of my replies. In a romantic gesture and in true Aubrey style, I believe he placed most of my letters alongside a *Time Life* book of the major events during the past century, and also some other items, in a time capsule.

This was my reply to his first or second letter.

* * * * *

December 16/1965

Dear Brey,

I never thought being around so many familiar people could be so lonely. How I miss you, strangely, we hardly spent much time together but those stolen hours felt like a beautiful lifetime. There is so much I want to say, I just don't know how! I hope in time I'll be able to express my feelings, for now all I can say is I love and think of you constantly. The girls at work tease me, especially when I receive a letter. I don't mind the teasing but never see any humour in it.

Went to visit Mater yesterday. I go there quite often, I feel close to you when I'm there. Your Dad and I exchange books and have discussions about them, I find him an interesting man and by no means intimidating. Not looking forward to the holidays especially Xmas Eve, the memories too vivid and painful. Helga, Cloe and I are taking the cubs to St. Ann's Orphanage, we bought some toiletries and sweets for the kids, Michael and the scouts will also be joining us. Our Christmas staff party is as

usual at the sports club, Ann wants me to attend with her, I haven't decided. Remember the last one? I got all dressed up for the party and you and I exchanged presents and spent the time together instead. How about you, what are your plans for the season?
   Will close now with love and hope to hear from you soon.

Love,
Merle

Aubrey and I sometimes exchanged our presents on Christmas Eve or when I could get away. We rode our bicycles alongside each other and a block before my home we stopped on the street and exchanged gifts. We then pushed our bikes as close as possible to my home so we could have a few more minutes together. Sometimes we exchanged at a friend's place, I never wanted to go to his home on Christmas Eve and we didn't dare go somewhere public.

His first letter in the New Year.

* * * * *

January 4/1966

Hello Love,

Tell me how much you miss me. How much? More than how I miss you. I do not believe you because if you did you surely would have written a few lines. Ah! do not become annoyed. I can hear you muttering that it was my turn to write. I agree with you but darling, I did not write before because I am working long hours trying to build a good bank account so that I could send for you. So, love, whenever you have some spare time, drop me a line so that I will not feel I am working in vain.

I am happy with my new job. It has an atmosphere of home, there are about 20 Guyanese employed but the reason I like it is mainly because of the salary. Some weeks I earn over $130. But I do not rest on my laurels and demand it, for me to earn that sort of money I have to sacrifice a lot of spare time, some Saturdays and at least one evening. I don't mind the extra hours of work. It's for us. I think you will like it here.

I am awaiting the day when you'll join me. Please do not let me down, when the time comes, if for any reason, such as love for your parents, somebody new, or uncertainty in your love for me and you feel you do not want to come any more, please let me know. Remember the foundation for a true and lasting relationship is loyalty and honesty, our friendship was built on this and if it is to continue, I want it to be on the same basis. So darling, if you have any doubts about our love, if you are now attracted to someone else, let me know. As for myself, I know I am not capable of loving anyone other than you.

Until my love, and write as often as possible, I have so little spare time. Take care and God bless you.

Yours forever,
Brey

By then I dared to believe in the possibility of us being married. Hope is indeed uplifting, it helps you dream and plan. We couldn't wait to be together. I recall thinking, "How I love this feeling, all of my waking hours are occupied with thoughts of Brey." I was totally ecstatic.

Aubrey started to save earnestly with the intention of sponsoring me as his fiancée. All our plans had to be kept a secret. His letters came to my office where I read them a few times, resealed the envelopes, and then gave them to my friend Marie to keep. Ma or Pa never looked through my personal belongings but I didn't want to take any chances. At that point, my life seemed to revolve around receiving and writing letters.

* * * * *

February 14/1966

My Dearest,

I received your letter and Valentine card, I am ashamed for not sending a card on your 21st birthday, I really wanted to very much, but girl I am always so tired in the evenings when I arrive home. I hope you will not hold

Some of Aubrey's letters

this against me. Please try to understand, it is not that I don't care, apart from working long hours, I am trying to adjust to life here, and some days are difficult and lonely. By now you must have gathered I am homesick. I miss the old lady, old man, Laureen, Philip, my drunken friends and most of all, you my love. You asked how much I miss you, to tell you the truth, it is extremely hard to express how much but what I can say is I miss and need you very much. I need you physically, as well as a mental pillar to lean on when I find myself in this frame of mind. I will tell you what I would do with you if you were here with me. You don't have to read any further but if I know that mind you possess, you'll read on, I would ————— . Incidentally, this is how I feel, tell me the truth, you'll love it, won't you?

So much for that, now for a few tit bits, the weather is still cold and lousy. I'll be visiting Joan and Collin this weekend. My dearest, I wish you a happy Valentine, and hope you'll always be my Valentine. Do not worry my love, I'll make up for all these injustices. Remember, I love you and always will. I close with all my love and lots of kisses. There is no truer or purer love than ours.

Take care of yourself,

Yours always,
Brey

That was the beginning of not receiving many cards from him. In all our years together, Aubrey must have sent me only a couple of dozen cards. When I teased him about this, he said the ones he gave me were timeless and chosen with much thought and all I have to do was read them year after year. He claimed, "My love for you never falters, so why another card to repeat what I always feel?" One lucky year, I received a wedding anniversary card for my birthday. He couldn't find a birthday card that expressed what he wanted to say and the anniversary card said it all. Another birthday, a friendship one. I must say that his cards, however infrequent, were indeed eloquently written.

On our first Valentine's Day as a married couple, I bought him a whimsical card, intending to inscribe and mail it from the office. I forgot it on my night table at home, so that evening I tucked the card into my handbag. The next morning, I took it out of the envelope at work, ready to write my message but Aubrey had beaten me to it. He had written, "To my dearest wife, from your ever-loving husband, Brey".

NINE

During the Easter of 1966, our scouts and cubs were going camping to Bartica. 'Bartica' is an Amerindian word for the red earth found throughout the region. This rugged terrain, off the Essequibo River, is also the gateway to the interior and is known for its annual regatta. I wrote Aubrey about the trip and he asked that I write prior to leaving and to be careful.

The second day after our arrival, we were hiking along a very rough path when a policeman driving a jeep offered us a ride. The pathway was narrow and littered with large rocks. Driving was treacherous and we ended up in a ditch. I was the only one injured because my arms were protecting a little boy in my lap during the collision. My head collided with the Jeep's metal crossbar, cutting my forehead which required thirteen stitches. I was hospitalised for a couple of days and refused to be flown home. Needless to say, the remaining week was a bit quiet and I survived on lots of pain killers.

When I returned to the city, and at my parents' insistence, more x- rays were done. I stayed at home reluctantly, while awaiting the results. I felt fine and wanted to return to work in case a letter was there from Aubrey. It so happened there was one. He had not heard from me for a while and was feeling a little unsure of our relationship.

* * * * *

April 17/1966

My Little Nastyface,

I trust you enjoyed your trip to Bartica for it most likely will be your last, hopefully you'll be here soon. Merle, if you know you will not be able to go through with our plans, please let me know now. Please do not wait until everything is finalised and then decide you cannot make it. In one of your letters you stated our happiness and being together was all that mattered, if you really meant this, then please do not hesitate to join me here, I miss you so much that the last thing I do before falling asleep is look at your pictures and hang on to my memories of you, silly is it not? But honestly, I miss you much more than I expected.

Well, let's get down to some serious business. Are you sure your parents will allow you to come to a strange country and to someone who is just a friend? If you are sure they will, then go ahead with our plans. I suggest Joan write you, inviting you to stay with her and Collin, Pa and Ma should read the letter, hopefully, you can get their comments and reaction. Let Joan emphasise that Toronto is better than Montreal regarding language, living and working conditions. I know your parents would settle in Montreal. I hope Joan will do her bit to help us. I will be visiting them this weekend to discuss everything in detail, you in the meantime, write to her as early as possible. I will be applying for you next month, so do not delay.

Should your parents allow Joan and Collin to look after you, I will then inform immigration to forward all correspondence to your home, if not then in care of D. Miller, so let me know asap what address to use. In the meantime, send your birth certificate, police clearance *and your passport number, you will also have to declare how much money you intend to bring with you, don't worry about that, I will send whatever is needed. I will also book your passage from here. I almost forgot, you will have to give a brief work experience, the type of Bookkeeping machine you operate etc.*

Remember love, do not discuss our plans with anyone.

So long until I hear from you, have courage.

Always Yours,
Brey

Aubrey was never sure of my commitment until we were married; he knew I loved him but how far was I willing to go to prove it? He was also aware of how much my parents' approval meant to me.

Prior to him leaving for Canada, we rarely discussed a future together, too much time was spent on enjoying each other's company and how to meet discreetly. After he departed I also felt unsure of his commitment sometimes, especially when his replies were delayed. In the meantime, I was corresponding with our friends, Joan and Collin who were residing in Toronto.

Ma knew of Joan and thought when I eventually go to Canada I would be spending some time with her. Joan and Collin were aware of our plans and offered to help in any way possible. Aubrey visited them often, apart from being friends, he and Joan were related; they shared a great grandmother.

By then my parents were planning to emigrate to Montreal and of course, I was to join them eventually. They thought I was applying on my own and would have no difficulties, because my brother Kash and his family resided there, I told them Toronto may be a better place to settle because of it being an English province, Ma and Pa had no idea it was all because

Aubrey and Collin in Toronto, 1966

of Aubrey and nothing to do with language. After promising four years ago not to associate with him anymore they must have thought our brief relationship was long over. They approved of me staying with Joan and Collin for a while and never suspected Aubrey was in Canada. A month later, I replied to the above letter, telling Aubrey about my accident.

He wrote the following.

* * * * *

June 5/1966

Hello Dearest,

I feel terrible, more so this time because of your accident. I should have written again when I did not hear from you. And have more faith rather than assuming you were no longer interested in me, this assumption, only because I know how guilty you feel about deceiving your parents and the influence they have over you. I guess I'll always feel this way, until you are here with me.

I was shocked to read about your accident, how is your wound healing and how are you feeling? I hope you are much better. All these injustices I am committing now I will make amends when we are together. Please darling, do not feel I do not love you because I do not write as often as I should. I love you and always will. I cannot give you a date as to when you'll be coming but I can assure you it will be before Christmas, just trust me.

My Merle, how I miss you, otherwise I'm fine, though certainly not happy. The weather has warmed up a bit, luckily our apartment is air conditioned. Your birth certificate and other papers arrived safely.

So long my love and be careful.

Love always,
Brey

TEN

Sometime in July 1966, my parents had to get their medicals done in preparation for emigrating to Canada and they hoped I would be approved by immigration around the same time so we would leave together, they to Montreal where my brother and his family resided and I to Toronto for a few days, eventually joining them.

My concern was that if my sponsorship through Aubrey wasn't approved soon, I would end up in Montreal.

This was his reply to my letter of concern.

* * * * *

July 13/1966

My Love,

I received your letter this evening when I got in from work. You stated you were worried because of the latest development regarding Ma and Pa coming here and you may have to join them in Montreal. Well, I will first say, don't panic. I will give you a few details that should put your mind at ease. Before I do this, I would like you to take your passport out of Ma and Pa's reaching and place it in a safe place, give it to Mater if you like, I advise this because if your passport is not in your possession, you will never be able to leave Guyana. So please do this now. And always remember, I love you. Ma and Pa will not leave until sometime in September, as I see it they will probably leave late September or early October, this is usually the time it takes to process everything, I can assure you, by then you will receive your medicals.

So darling do not worry, everything will be just fine. I will be applying for you next week, I didn't do so earlier because I was trying to build up my bank account, to date I have over $600. You should hear from immigration before the end of August. Because I'll be applying for you as my fiancée, immigration will expedite your papers without much delay. Love, your parents will never be able to sponsor you or for that matter, anyone before next year and by then you will be over here as 'Mrs Merle Miller'. My darling, Ma and Pa are living their lives, do not let them live yours for you.

So long my love, until I hear from you.

Yours always,
Brey

After that above letter of assurance, some time passed without any correspondence and I started to worry. I wondered if Aubrey was having second thoughts and, being a gentleman, was going along with the hope that I would eventually back out, which he always felt was possible. I wrote him expressing my concern and indicated it was alright if he was having doubts about his commitment to me. Big mistake!

This was his reply.

Georgetown, 1966

* * * * *

October 22/1966

Hello you of little faith,

Received your letter and I must say I am somewhat disappointed in you. How could you for one moment think, much less believe what you wrote. I just cannot see how you came to such conclusions, when I never gave you any reason to think the way you did. After four years you do not seem to have any faith or trust in me. To be honest, I am surprised to think you felt I had deserted you or I was marrying you through pangs of a guilty conscience. Well, let me tell you now, if you honestly believe I am in love with someone else, or that I am marrying you not because I love you but because I feel I owe you this, I would advise you not to pursue any further with our plans.

I must add here and now, what you wrote, none of it is true. Always believe this and never doubt any part of it any time. Whether you marry me or not, I love you and always will. My love will always be yours, no other girl could compare with you. You are sweet, honest, delightful and everything any man would want. How ridiculous can you be to produce such thoughts! I would love to get hold of you right now and ─────.prove how wrong your thoughts are of me. When you come over, I will take one week off work and we will have a week of fun and laughter. I plan to have you ─────. Just imagine, my innocent little Merle indulging in ───── ──. Do you realise the end of this month will be five years we have loved each other?

    Well love, I cannot imagine you weighing **96 pounds**, *I like that.*

I will close now with all my love.
Love, Brey

Feeling confident and reassured, I enclosed some pictures of myself in a pool with my next letter. In his response, Aubrey reminded me to be careful as two of his cousins drowned while swimming and he thought I was too impulsive and accident prone. Apart from my head injury in Bartica, my only other accident was with a friend who was teaching me how to ride his motorcycle. Of course, when Ma and Pa were out.

    What a night that was! The street was deserted and I wanted to have a go on the bike. I did not take a wide enough turn and the back wheel skidded out and both Andrew and I fell with the bike, the exhaust pipe rested on my calf and burnt it badly. I was terrified of telling my parents and endured the pain throughout the night. The next morning Ma had a fit when she saw my calf and we immediately went to the hospital. They were too worried to reprimand me. That burn took many months to heal.

    Despite my mishaps, our correspondence kept up.

* * * * *

November 9/1966

Hello Love,

I received your letter containing the pictures. I must say they certainly are lovely, especially the one you crossed at the back, you look so sexy. Love, do be careful with your swimming, remember you are accident prone and I do not think I could stand anything happening to you, especially being so far away. So please, be careful.

Darling, I have a favour to ask and I hope you will grant my request. Please do not cut your hair, I love it long. You look so lovely and desirable in your pictures. Looking at them just reminds me of how much I love you. And I shudder at the thought of ever losing you.

I have forwarded all the necessary papers to immigration and I expect you'll be here in about four months; this cannot be too soon. Presently, it is raining quite heavily. If you were here I would —————. Love, it is situations like this that makes me feel the need for you, so we could talk things over.

Today I was offered a job with IBM. Apart from the money, it could lead to a career in electronics, it is a world-renowned firm with lots of possibilities. I will be trained to build computers used in laboratories, hospitals, banks etc. Really, to be honest it is a once in a lifetime opportunity. I have the job if I want it, I wrote the test passed and was offered the position today. And you know what, I am going to refuse it, you are puzzled as to why. Should I take it, with the demand for computers, I would be working in the evenings for a period of two or three years. They work round the clock. We would be married early next year and for me to take a job that warrants my working at night, well, I do not think it would be good for our marriage. When you leave for work in the mornings, I would be asleep. When you arrive home in the evenings, I'll be at work. So, you see, the only time we would be together is on the weekends. Babe, I'm not marrying you to be with you only on weekends, I am marrying you because I want to be with you as much as possible. So, to hell with the job, I want my Merle. I know you are thinking that later I might regret this, let me assure you, all I want in life is to be with you, my only regret would be not spending enough time with you.

I asked what size you wear, because I want to send away for a negligée I saw in a catalogue. I should have known a small. Thanks for the shirts, I have not tried them on but I'm sure they will fit.

Well love, I think that's all for now, I close with my love. Hello to Lovin and Yvonne. Take care of yourself and my love always,

Brey

* * * * *

November 13/1966

My Dearest,

I do not know when this letter will reach you for Air Canada is due to go on strike from tomorrow and a postal strike is threatening to start on the 15th Nov., but I feel like writing, so here goes.

I noticed in your letter you stated you did not like my last letter because it was not passionate enough. What I will do is write half passionate and half business like. First business, I hope you do not mind getting married in the Catholic Church, I am not asking, nor will I ever ask you to give up your religion for mine. I had for the purpose of immigration, have a priest sign a document *stating arrangements have been made for our wedding. Please let me know what your thoughts are about it. Speaking about immigration, they informed me you would be hearing from them soon, depending on the strike. Love, I think we should be together within four months. Yesterday I was downtown and saw a beautiful engagement and wedding band set, I think you will like it. As soon as you arrive, we'll check it out.*

If you think some of my letters are sexy, I should write exactly how I feel, bold and clear but they will be too hot to be read by my little naive girl. Love if you know how often I lay in bed and dream of when we are together and ——————. My darling, I have come to love and want you more than any man has the right to want a woman. I will try my best to be the perfect husband. I seem to live just for you.

I close with all my love,
Brey

* * * * *

November 28/1966

Hello Love,

Just a short note to let you know I received your letter informing me about your medicals. I am overjoyed at hearing this and hope you will forward the results asap. Well, I have done my part and it is now up to you to make a five year dream a reality.

I was thinking of you last night and as to how much I love you and why. Let's face it, you have the components of any normal woman on a physical basis. You have the bulges and curves in the right areas. This is important but not as important as your other attributes that have attracted me to you. What I see in you are a combination of factors that I found lacking in some people and yet is a vital ingredient for living a fulfilling life.

I love you because you are kind, loyal, proud and have integrity. Love I want to marry you because I feel you are all of the above. You may have noticed that most of my letters are filled with how I want you physically, it is not that I want you in this respect only. I think most women like to know they are physically attractive and never get tired of hearing it. I want you to be my wife because I love you more than anyone or anything and feel we are good for each other. I know I may not be the best catch but always remember, I will do my best where you are concerned.

Just wanted you to know why I think you are so special.

I am eagerly awaiting the day when you arrive here. Please do not cut your hair.

Love, Brey

ELEVEN

Christmas of 1966 was incredibly sad and confusing. I was sure I loved Aubrey and wanted to spend the rest of my life with him but was our love strong enough to endure what lay ahead? After the security, comfort and love, not only from my parents but also my siblings, I started to doubt my decision and worried about how wrong things could go. No support from my family, a new country and committed to marrying the only man I'd ever dated.

Ma and Pa noticed my sadness and thought I was missing my sister and cousin. Zorena had moved to England and Yvonne's father was transferred to Berbice. Both girls knew Aubrey and I loved each other but nothing of our plans. I eventually wrote to Yvonne, who left Guyana a few months later for England. I told her not to share this information with anyone. The only other folks who knew of our plans were Aubrey's parents and two friends from the office. My parents tried their best to cheer me up, surprisingly Pa even encouraged me to attend a party at a friend's home, which I declined.

Another friend, Zam, received a Triumph convertible car for Christmas from his parents and he came around on Christmas day to take me out for a drive. Ma and Pa had no objections. As we were driving towards the east coast, parallel to the Atlantic Ocean, and while enjoying the cool breeze against my face, I thought for a moment: *Pa readily agreed for me to go driving with Zam and would have welcomed a romantic relationship.* Ma knew Zam's mother and some folks thought we would be a good match. In reality, he and I were simply good friends and we both enjoyed dancing. Zam also knew briefly about my interest in Aubrey. I felt obligated to confide in him when he once tried to convey "goodnight" with a kiss that I didn't consider platonic.

While sitting in the car next to him, I thought. "If only it was Aubrey driving, how ecstatic I would have been." I dismissed those wasted longings and tried to concentrate on Zam's elation about his new wheels.

By now you would have thought I had grown accustomed to the guilt and deception, but this was not the case. Although Aubrey and I had been in love for over four years, I was still uncomfortable deceiving my parents.

Whenever I felt worried, confused or uncertain, my replies to his letters were delayed, simply because I just didn't know what to say. He must have sensed this and wrote the following, which was his last letter of 1966.

* * * * *

December 18/1966

My dearest,

Just a short note to let you know how much I love you and am patiently awaiting your arrival. Before I go any further, let me wish you a Merry Christmas and a Happy New Year! I received your card and must say it is lovely.

Thought by now I would have heard from you. How was your medicals, have you completed it and returned the results to immigration? Let me know when you receive your visa, this should be around mid January, I will book your passage upon hearing from you.

Love, please do not let me down, if you do not come to me, I will have no alternative but to come and get you. I am serious. I know I am asking a lot of you. To leave your parents with the possibility of never seeing them again, is indeed too much to ask. But I ask this because I am prepared to devote my life to making you happy and I hope one day your parents will accept the situation.

When the time comes, and you are caught between indecisions, remember

(1) Decide on what you want and stick to it, regardless of the consequences.

(2) Your decision not to come could very well have far reaching consequences for both of us.

(3) I have loved you for five years and will continue to do so for the rest of my life.

I know you enjoyed reading my last letter, I meant every word. I can't wait to ─────────.

I suggest you start preparing to travel. Have your smallpox vaccine as soon as possible, if all goes well you may have only six weeks left. I am going to book a direct flight, no overnighting at the stops.

Well love, that's all for now, continue to have faith in us, and all will be well. Have a Merry Christmas and remember, I love you.

Yours always,
Brey

Letters like the above always restored my confidence that I was doing the right thing but as the time drew nearer, I felt scared about everything. This was indeed a big step in my life and the uncertainties were enormous. Apart from the taboo of living with Aubrey, prior to getting married, I was going to meet and share a home with his aunt and uncle whom I had never met. I took a long time replying to the above letter, simply because of all the turmoil I was experiencing.

My parents' visa came through and they left three weeks ahead of me. I stayed with family friends, as my only sibling left in Guyana was Khalda, and she lived in Essequibo. Ma and Pa left with the knowledge that I would go to Toronto and then on to Montreal.

Aubrey wrote a couple more letters, then this, his last one, just prior to my departure.

*****

February 6/1967

Hello Love,

Received your letter and I am pleased to hear your visa has come through. After my interview with immigration on the 24th Jan. I wanted to book your passage but did not do so because I was not sure when the visa would have been forwarded. I will book it for the 5th March, you can hand in your resignation. As soon as your flight is confirmed I will forward all the details. Are you sure you do not want me to send you any money, please don't be shy about it. I am going to forward some anyway.

Why are your letters of late so cold? They give me the impression that you are not very enthusiastic about the whole matter. If you feel you are doing the wrong thing or if you have the slightest doubt, now is the time to call it off. As for myself I am sure beyond any shadow of doubt that I want to spend the rest of my life with you. A few months ago your letters made me feel you were anxious to be here with me. Now they are short, cold and on the whole not very encouraging. I hope I am reading more into it and that you still want to marry me. Personally, I think you might have to be married in a suit. You see it will be rather cold and you would have to wear a winter coat which may be a bit of a bother with a wedding gown and snow, anyhow the decision is yours.

I wish you a happy birthday and that's all for now until I hear from you.

Love, Brey
PS. I love you

I don't think I ever told Aubrey how torn I felt during the months of January and February 1967. My love for him and my loyalty to Ma and Pa were in conflict. After so many years, I still couldn't deal with it. I wasn't brave enough to confront my parents or strong enough to forgo my love for Aubrey. Constantly plagued by my guilty conscience, I was also afraid of being alienated from my family, or maybe getting cold feet at the thought of living with strangers and fending for myself. The worst part was having no one to confide in, to get advice from, or just tell me I was making the right decision by following my heart. I felt lost, alone, and totally miserable and I guess that was conveyed in my letters. However, I continued with preparations, even as my emotions switched between elation and sadness within minutes.

As it turned out, I did get to wear a wedding gown, made for me by Aubrey's Mom. Mater was adamant I wear a dress and not a suit for the ceremony. My bridal gown was made from French *peau de soie* and Swiss *guipure* and it fitted beautifully. Mater also made me a new wardrobe for my new life in Canada.

One day Mr Miller asked me to join him in their living room and said, "It seems as if my son and you are going to be married. I have a gold sovereign and want to make a wedding ring out of it for Aubrey to give you." Being too young to appreciate the honour, I refused. "No thanks, I think it is Aubrey's place to get my ring." I couldn't read his reaction but he seemed slightly taken aback. Mater later told me that a lot of sentiment was attached to that sovereign and he must really like me to make such an offer. Sometime later, Mr Miller approached me regarding a departure gift and asked what I would like. I told him a suitcase and we decided to meet at a certain store so I could select my gift. With all that was on my mind, I completely forgot and the dear man waited way beyond our scheduled time.

A couple of days later I visited them and was informed by their cook, Linda, that one does not keep the 'Governor' (her secret name for him) waiting and he was in the living room. I greeted Mr Miller and apologised. He was not satisfied with my humble apology and claimed irritatedly, "You! You slip of a girl, kept me waiting for over an hour!" My thoughts were too occupied at that moment with uncertainties to worry about the Governor's irritation or lack of a suitcase. I don't recall if I excused myself, or was dismissed, as I joined Mater and proceeded to discuss my wardrobe. Aubrey's dad rescheduled our luggage appointment and I displayed a huge reminder on my desk. So large that everyone in the office knew I was meeting a "Mr Miller at 11:45am". We met, I selected my suitcase and all was well.

On the day of my departure, my sister Khalda travelled to the city to help where necessary and to see me off. I placed my wedding gown at the bottom of the suitcase, hoping she would not see it. By the time she arrived my case was nearly packed. I remember holding on to her and crying when we said goodbye. I so wanted to tell her of my plans but was scared and still distraught about my decision.

TWELVE

I boarded the plane and as it took flight, I watched the landscape of Guyana disappear and thought, "What the hell am I doing here?" The realisation of my decision started to settle in. I was venturing out to Canada to marry Aubrey, without my parents' knowledge. I guess 'elope' was the right term, my fervent imagination was rampant. Do I really love this man? Can I trust him? I'll be in a vulnerable situation. Should things go wrong, what am I going to do? Marriage is a lifetime commitment. We never spent much time together to plan our future. What is the criteria for a successful marriage? Loyalty, trust, respect and, of course, the main ingredient, love; not forgetting admiration. What a time and place for doubts and second thoughts. The only thing I was sure of was my adoration for him, and how he made my heart beat faster. I prayed for guidance and also remembered asking God to forgive me for the hurt and disappointment I would cause my parents.

The flight to Canada was long enough for me to continue reflecting on my life and where the future would take me. I was scared, curious, naive, trusting and alienating myself from the people I loved and with whom I felt safe. Little did I know of the turmoil to follow, which included ignorance, guilt, heartache and to top it all, a good bout of chickenpox.

After six hours of trepidation and no sleep, we eventually arrived at JFK airport in New York, just before midnight. Aubrey suggested I call him during the short stop over. Sitting next to me in the terminal was a young man trying to engage in conversation. I kept ignoring him, I was too busy looking for the down escalator. By then I knew the phones were on the upper floor. I could see how to get up to the next level but was concerned as to how to get back down. You see, this was my first encounter with escalators, we didn't have any in Guyana and I vaguely remember seeing them in movies, all between our stolen kisses. I eventually told the Brazilian – sometime during his rambling, I remember hearing 'Brazil' – I was looking for a phone. He offered to accompany me upstairs and waited while I spoke with Aubrey, then escorted me around the bend to the 'down' escalator. He then politely bid me adieu. I guess he couldn't avoid overhearing my part of the conversation and realised his kind offer would lead to nothing more than just, 'a kind offer.'

I arrived in Toronto at about 3am. Aubrey and I had been apart for sixteen months. When we held each other, it felt so good. I was elated and remember thinking, "This is where I belong!" However, this feeling of 'belonging' lasted just about the time it took us to arrive at the two-bedroom apartment he shared with his aunt and uncle.

After the usual introductions, they were warm and welcoming. We chatted for a while, then Aubrey guided me to our bedroom which was fully furnished with a double bed. Reality then stepped in and my first question was, "Where am I going to sleep?" Upon seeing the look on my face, he assured me the bed was for sleeping and nothing else, unless I chose otherwise. 'Nothing else' lasted twenty-eight days; that's how long it took us to get married. I didn't want a civil ceremony. With all the guilt and deception plaguing me, I wanted someone who had a better relationship with God to bless our marriage. Unfortunately, the priest with whom Aubrey had made all the arrangements with was away on a month's skiing holiday, which delayed our ceremony. In the meantime, Ma and Pa thought I was visiting with my friends Joan and Collin in Toronto before moving to Montreal.

Sometime within the twenty-eight days, I decided to change the status of my upcoming marriage from 'elopement' to 'parents' knowledge, without blessing'. I felt dishonest and deeply unhappy. Being with Aubrey and so much in love was not enough. It seemed I was living a double life. I had to tell Ma and Pa but how and when?

I spoke with them often and they were anxiously awaiting my arrival in Montreal. Lying to my parents and giving the impression I would eventually move there made me feel totally distraught. All the effort to be with Aubrey while in Guyana suddenly seemed merely a little daring and happy. After my secret rendezvous with him, I returned to a safe haven with my family. Now I was on my own, living with strangers and marrying without my parents' blessing, all within a few weeks. I was overcome with guilt, doubt and I was totally confused. Aubrey never tried to influence me in any way and would just hold me while assuring me of his love and protection, as I cried myself to sleep many nights.

One may think, why all the unhappiness and indecision? After all, I was an adult and could legally do as I wish, but family expectations and loyalty were enormous obstacles. Our family is very close; anything that would displease or hurt my parents bothered me. During one of our telephone conversations, I told Ma I was interested in a guy here in Toronto and was considering staying. I would however, visit them in Montreal soon. She never asked his name or where he was from and was upset with me. I was promptly told to get on the next train to Montreal. After that conversation I didn't call for over a week, I just dreaded speaking with them.

All through my loving Aubrey, confronting my parents with anything concerning him was my biggest problem. I was such a coward. Until one morning after another sleepless night, I suddenly sat up in bed, woke Aubrey and told him I was going to Montreal to discuss everything with my parents. He did not try to persuade me otherwise, but just hoped I was emotionally strong enough to reason with them. He knew between the guilt, love and loyalty to Ma and Pa, I may be persuaded to remain there for a while; long enough for them to ask me to reconsider the situation, with the hope I would change my mind. Which was exactly what Ma tried to do.

Aubrey saw me off at Union Station, where we hugged a little longer and tighter but said nothing. As my dreaded rail journey started, I watched the landscape pass by and thought, "This looks the way I feel, cold, flat and dismal with dark clouds". After what seemed like an endless ride of troubled thoughts and no rest, I arrived at Gare Centrale feeling worse for the crowd and noise and missing the quiet safety of Aubrey more than ever.

My brother Kash met me at the train station and we chatted about everything except my reason for coming to Montreal. I sensed he knew how uneasy I felt and just wanted to help me relax. I presumed all that he knew about the situation, was my interest in a man in Toronto. In the car we kept our conversation light and casual, while my stomach churned; not from lack of food, but the dreaded confrontation with my parents. During our last conversation, just prior to departing for Montreal, I told them Aubrey Miller was the person I loved. I had no intention of telling them over the phone and really don't remember why I blurted out that crucial bit of information at that untimely moment. So, they too must have been apprehensive about our meeting. Though I doubted they remembered who Aubrey Miller was; he had visited our home only once. Then there was the time Zed told them about Aubrey and I being at the movies. These two incidents occurred over five years ago.

Upon arrival, I was greeted first by my sister-in-law, Glad, then Pa and Ma. Just a tight hug from Pa, his silence lasted the duration of my visit. Ma was all over me, commenting how thin I was and immediately ready with food. Whenever I am worried or upset, my appetite wanes; Ma remembered this. She guided me to the table and in a gentle, persuasive voice said, "You may not feel like eating but try just a little bit." I did to please her, then went for a shower. I later joined them in the living room and revealed everything. I declared my love for Aubrey and my intention to marry him. I also apologised for the deception. Much to my surprise, they remembered him! The cliché, 'All hell broke loose' described the situation. Ma and I talked and cried at the same time, Pa's stoic expression scared me and I was oblivious as to where Kash or Glad were at that moment. They later joined us, and my brother was torn between our parents and me.

Ma cajoled, bribed, spoke a few octaves higher at times and tried to cut a deal with me. I distinctly remember their compromise. They would send me anywhere I chose for a year. After that period, should I still want to marry Aubrey, they would give their blessing. She also insinuated my feelings for him were just infatuation and being apart would take care of the situation. Two things were wrong with their offer. Firstly, the Canadian immigration expected us to marry within a month of my arrival and secondly, my parents had no idea how intense my love for Aubrey was and being away from him again, for any amount of time, was inconceivable. When I looked at Pa, who continued the silent treatment for my entire four days visit, I thought, "My dear arrogant father, always in control, now reduced to this quiet man." How I longed for some sort of reaction, approval, or just a smile from him. He sat on a chair, hands clasped and stared at the floor, while my mother laid down all the stipulations.

I must add that during my entire visit, they never said anything negative about Aubrey, apart from Ma's relentless objection with me marrying him without knowing much, except that he was not of East Indian descent. Quoting her, "This contention has nothing to do with Aubrey Miller, only with you. If you decide not to marry him, what could he possibly do?" Even though my parents' blessing meant so much, loving Aubrey took precedence. After refusing their offer, I departed amidst continued silence from Pa and tears from Ma. I cried all the way to Toronto. Though, throughout my weeping I remember feeling profoundly sad, but less guilty.

Sitting next to me on the train was an older gentleman who tried some small talk about the weather and an occasional smile, while I'm sure wondering why so many tears. He even offered to share his lunch with me. The dear man had no idea that even after a sleepless night and five hours on the train, food was not an option or consolation, and definitely the last thing on my mind. I imagine Aubrey was relieved to see me back, though I was too unhappy and torn to notice. I just clung to him silently for a few minutes, then had a shower and went to bed. While staring at the ceiling, I kept seeing Ma's face as she leaned against the door crying when I departed, and prayed that one day my parents would forgive me for hurting them.

My betrayal was loving Aubrey, and I hoped our love was worth the alienation and heartache I was feeling. Only time would tell!

THIRTEEN

By then, all six of my siblings knew about my forbidden love. I started to receive telegrams from Arif; those few lines of support were most comforting. Years later, Zorena told me that he had also written to our parents trying to convince them to give their blessing. From my other siblings there was not much. I don't think it was because they objected, they just couldn't convince my parents otherwise.

Khalda, my only sibling still residing in Guyana, kept me informed through correspondence about Ma and Pa, who by then had cut off all communication with me. That was the toughest part of my ordeal. I could cope with their anger and hostility, but the silence was devastating. My many telephone calls were unanswered and I thought to continue calling would have made matters worse. They were adamant and my calls would only aggravate the situation. I also wrote a few letters which were not acknowledged. I eventually accepted their decision with much regret and unhappiness.

The priest returned from his skiing trip with no broken bones. I thanked God! Another delay would have driven me away from both Aubrey and my parents. By then I was emotionally exhausted, confused and, at times, questioned my decision about marrying him.

We had a meeting with the Father to finalise the arrangements for our marriage. He wanted to speak with me alone and came right to the point, by asking if I would convert to Catholicism. I told him no, which he thought was because

I was a Muslim. I explained, "Father, I don't believe in the customs and rituals of Catholicism or Islam. My religion is just between God and me." There was no comment from the priest.

We re-joined Aubrey and when asked about contraceptives, we admitted we weren't ready for a family. We had other plans for the next three to four years, like working and saving enough for Aubrey to attend university. However, we promised when we eventually start a family, our babies would be baptised in the Catholic Church; a commitment we kept. Aliya and Tazra married Catholics and our grandchildren are also of the faith. The Father got so much more than he expected.

We were married on Monday, April 3rd 1967 at 7:30pm. A "Twilight Wedding" it was referred as; a highly overrated description, for it was beyond twilight, and a wet wintery evening. I cried all through the ceremony, the priest waited patiently while I repeated my vows between sobs. Yes, I did a lot of weeping in 1967. Total guests were approximately ten or twelve. Half of them I didn't know, our closest friends Joan and Collin were unable to attend. The wedding feast was KFC with all the side dishes but I had no appetite, even if it had been chateaubriand and lobster. Mater insisted on making a traditional Guyanese wedding cake, just a little round fruit and rum cake which I had brought with me and had decorated in Toronto.

After loving each other for five years, we did not consummate our marriage that night. I had gotten my period the previous day although it was not due; maybe the stress brought it on. Another night of Aubrey just holding me! However, a week later I lived the passion, when my body and soul became aware of such splendour! I believe the ultimate vulnerability is when you trust your partner. I surrendered, totally! Even after feeling ecstatically quenched, I held on, caressed, tears flowed and I felt complete. The physical part of a relationship is important and so piquant. But the soul, in my opinion, is the core of all that is, it feels and endures.

Later, when we could barely be apart, I asked Aubrey how was he able to sleep in such close proximity and not try any

Our wedding day. Aubrey's uncle Raymond is in the background

amorous persuasion. He replied. "You had a lot going on and as much as I would have loved to, the timing was not right. Apart from that, you were brought up to wait until your wedding night and I was not going to persuade you otherwise, not even for the pinnacle of pleasure." As I reflect on my past, I think of the love, patience and understanding Aubrey exercised prior to and during our marriage and hope in his eyes I was worthy of his thoughtfulness, devotion and commitment. He did love well!

Within a month of being married, I contracted chicken pox and it spread everywhere. Aubrey took tender care of me, twice a day he patiently tended to each pox, ensuring minimum discomfort. During that period, I thought constantly of my parents and the care they exercised when my siblings and I were ill. Apart from doctors, they never let anyone else take care of us; Pa was every bit involved as Ma. How I missed them. I never mentioned to Aubrey the hours of weeping I did while he was at work, or the guilt I felt for all the happiness I shared with him. He always came home to a smiling face and ghastly-tasting food.

FOURTEEN

Settling into a new country and married life was exciting, challenging and sometimes sad. I was also adjusting to the climate, especially the freezing rain, my weather nightmare. Knowing this, Aubrey always told me to take extra care when stepping outside. After his passing, I derived great comfort in writing to him. Reminiscing our years together is sometimes distracting and makes grieving more bearable.

Here is one of the letters I wrote.

*****

February 24/2015

My darling Brey,

Another soul-searching day. This restless feeling, random memories, along with concerns about trivial chores invade my thoughts. My memories are vivid and I can't seem to contain them in a little corner of my brain, so I give myself free range to remember. I sit and reflect on the fifty-three years of knowing and loving you. Those years were beautiful and sometimes challenging. My darling we are no longer together but because we have shared so many moments, my heart and brain is forever busy with thoughts of us. Brey, I will always remember! These 'thoughts' allow me to relive moments I choose and regretfully, some I don't.

Days like today, I push away the chores. I have an appointment with Adam, but rescheduled it for next week. The weatherman predicted freezing rain, so my excuse is valid. Freezing rain, my weather nightmare. Remember my early days in Canada, how I fell every winter? You would call me from work, reminding me to be careful because it was icy out. I thought your phone calls may have jinxed me, for even with your warning, I always fell. Stepping outside, my body would hit the ice in postures unimaginable. While down, three concerns always flashed before me, all in a few seconds. Who has seen me, what was hurting, and the most worrisome, how to get back on my feet in a dignified manner. Luckily, they were all minor accidents. Then a couple of years later, we bought our first car; a brand new Pontiac for thirty-eight hundred dollars. My fear of falling was replaced with the horror of driving on ice. We will relive those driving days in another letter.

As expected, February is extremely cold. I wonder if you are aware of the happenings here. I will relate all anyhow, so indulge me.

Anyhow, back to reminiscence and my first winter with the milk incident. That cold day many winters ago, after getting off the bus from work, I went across the street to buy milk and ended up purchasing a few other items. Upon entering our apartment, I started to cry, claiming, "I want to go back home!" You replied gently, "Darling, you are home." I meant Guyana. After helping me get warm, you said you'll go and purchase the milk. That was when I remembered, I left it downstairs in the foyer. The bag was heavy, especially the milk, which came in four litre jugs. My fingers were cold, I put down my purchases and in my eagerness to get into the elevator, I forgot the bags. You went down for them. How patient and tolerant you were, helping me adjust to my new life.

Today, I ate my dinner while watching television. Something else I've discovered since you've gone, I dislike eating alone, another adjustment to get accustomed to. I rarely sit at the table; most times I sit with a plate on my lap and eat in front of the television.

Must close now, if not I'll be rambling on and on, though rest assured, you have not heard the last of me.

My love always and beyond,
Merle

Aubrey helped with the apartment cleaning and I tried extremely hard at preparing our meals. My culinary and general housekeeping skills were abominable and I had to learn from making a cup of tea to everything else. I burnt dishes and discarded pots into the garbage because they were so badly scorched; I couldn't scrub them clean enough. Whatever knowledge Aubrey acquired regarding maintaining a home, none of it was found in the kitchen. After over a year helping his aunt and uncle, he didn't learn much. I, in turn, was even worse. Our meals were constantly disastrous. We always ended up ordering in, after my attempts were deemed unfit for human consumption.

By then, I realised that preparing food took more skill and knowledge than I had anticipated or was capable of and decided to invest in a cookbook and measuring utensils. That book became our survival guide. It taught me everything from boiling an egg, to preparing a four-course meal. Regretfully, there was no recipe for making curry, a dish I enjoy but never mastered.

Then there was the laundry situation; how much detergent to use, what water temperature was suitable and how to sort colours. Not to mention the many trips back and forth in the elevator to the laundry room. My neighbour, after looking at my bewildered and frustrated face said, "Read the instructions on the labels, dear." I never told her I had cut most of them

Toronto, 1968

off because they irritated my skin. That day she kindly walked me through the water temperature of each item. I remember my obsession with saving quarters for many years, after the experience of not having one to finish drying our clothes; the wet laundry was hung everywhere in our little apartment. That was when I asked Aubrey, "Could we get help to do our laundry? Back home someone washed and ironed all our clothing and linens." He reminded me that we were not 'back home'. I again faced the astounding transformation of coping in a completely new and different lifestyle. It seemed that every day I had to learn a new chore. Laundry was then added to my list!

Despite the disasters involving cooking and other domestic chores, we laughed, talked and did crazy things, like going to an all-night drive-in and seeing four movies in one evening. Between snacking on junk food, necking and cat naps, I don't think we saw one movie from beginning to end. It seemed as if we did what folks do while dating, except, we dated after we were married.

One Friday afternoon, we packed a few necessities and drove to Connecticut where we spent the night with some friends, then went on to New York City. We shopped, dined, took in a play on Broadway and went to a little night club situated in what seemed like a basement dwelling in Greenwich Village and did not go to bed until way past 3am. Later that day we drove home to Toronto and then out to work on Monday.

Aubrey also taught me how to play poker. The stakes were, well, use your imagination. He won constantly and I remember feeling quite chilly while playing that particular game. I once suggested we change the ante, the loser drink a glass of water. While I was running back and forth to the bathroom, he looked at me in mock severity and suggested we revert to the previous bet, claiming I wouldn't have the inconvenience and he would enjoy both winning and the view. Scrabble was another favourite pastime; we were both avid readers and found it to be a challenging game, so much so, that we bought a travel version to play in our hotel room once the kids were settled for the night. We also played bridge in Riyadh; Aubrey was quite good at bridge, a skill he acquired in Guyana.

Sometime during the summer of 1968, about fifteen months into our marriage, my brother Zed and his family were visiting from California. They spent most of their time in Montreal with my parents, my brother and his family, and then came on to Toronto for a short visit with us. Because I hadn't kept in contact with some of my siblings since I married Aubrey, Zed didn't have our address or phone number and called every 'A. Miller' in the telephone directory. After many attempts, he dialled the right number and we connected. They came to our apartment and finally met Aubrey.

We spent the entire day together and during our conversation, my sister-in-law Lyla, told me that Ma and Pa were going through a lot of anguish and realised that they must either accept and welcome Aubrey, or continue to be alienated from me. That bit of information gave me some hope

Winter, 1971

and the remainder of their visit was a joyful experience. It did my heart good to have my eldest brother's blessing.

A few months later, my parents called and invited us to Montreal for the Christmas holidays. I think Zed and my other siblings had a hand in that. I had a cold and was not up to travelling, but decided to go for the New Year. We drove to Montreal with Joan and Collin, as Joan also had a brother there to visit. Ma and Pa welcomed us with hugs and smiles and one wouldn't think that such hurt, frustration and anger had ever been between us.

They were very warm towards Aubrey and asked if we had any objections to having our marriage blessed in a small Muslim ceremony. We happily agreed, so they invited a few of their friends and gave us a little reception after the blessing; they also gave us some money as a wedding present. That ceremony helped heal our relationship and after the visit, we spoke on the phone and visited often.

Years later, Ma admitted her misjudgement, "*Betee* (daughter in Hindi), I'm glad you disobeyed us. Aubrey is a wonderful husband and father, and you have the look of a happy and content woman." I asked her why they were so against him and she said that it was because they knew nothing of his family or background, also they were concerned about what their relatives and friends would think of me marrying outside of our religion and ethnicity. Incidentally, half of my siblings married out of our religion and ethnicity. They escaped the badgering because they were not living in Guyana at the time.

As it turned out, everyone welcomed Aubrey with open arms. By then they knew of his integrity, charm and grace. However, impatience and intolerance were also part of his personality, but as he was always the gentleman, I doubt they ever saw those traits.

When I think of all of the guilt, heartache and lying, I wondered if I should have been more honest with my parents and declared my love for Aubrey while still in Guyana. A couple of years after being married, he and I were on holiday there and I asked my sister Khalda if I had behaved thoughtlessly. She promptly said our parents would have sent me off to England to keep me away from him. That took care of my theory as to how I should have dealt with the situation.

FIFTEEN

As planned, after four years of saving for University and at the age of thirty, Aubrey quit his job and went back to school. Although he was a few years older than most of his classmates, he made close friends; especially one particular friend, whom he kept in touch with throughout his life.

At that time, we were also pregnant with Aliya. Aubrey and I shared nine months of wonder and joy. Upon leaving the doctor's office after being told I was pregnant, in my elation, I immediately went shopping and bought a sewing machine, a pattern, material and all the notions necessary to make myself a dress. Most of the maternity dresses in the shop windows looked tall and wide, and even in nine months they would be huge – I weighed just 105 pounds at the time. So I decided to try sewing my own. I followed the instructions, from threading the needle to cutting out the dress, while thinking, "This can't be too difficult."

I was six weeks pregnant when I started my project, and after eight months it was still incomplete. Noticing my frustration and despondency, Aubrey eventually came to my rescue by using his slide rule and pencil, instructing me where to rip and where to stitch. When we, or rather Aubrey completed my dress, it fitted beautifully, complementing my, by then, protruding tummy. The many late nights of keeping his mother's company while she worked, seemed to have paid off.

Both our parents were ecstatic about welcoming another grandchild and by then, Ma and Pa had moved to Toronto. I recall my father-in-law's way of suggesting we start a family earlier; he mailed us a little card with a toddler sitting on a rock with the inscription, "tempus" (time). Dad was indeed a thoughtful man. During my pregnancy, Mater made me beautiful maternity dresses and Dad mailed them individually as they were completed. I always thought Mater initiated this kind gesture, but years later she told me it was 'old man Miller'. He suggested the idea and covered the expenses for all the material and mailing. Regretfully, he passed away a few months after Aliya's birth, which he proudly announced in the Guyana newspaper. I'm sorry our girls never knew him, they would have shared and enjoyed many opinions, debates and I'm sure heated arguments. I think Dad would have been proud of them and they he.

Aliya was born on January 1st, 1972. The first time I held her in my arms I vowed that one day she would marry whomever she chose, with the hope they love and respect each other. I was so completely happy. I prayed my baby would experience the same relationship in her life. I stayed home to take care of her. Those were rough years. With no income the savings depleted quickly. However, between student loans, grants, and Aubrey working at his former job every summer, we survived. Aubrey's brother Richard, an accountant, did the books for a couple of companies and he was able to give me a few hours of work from home, which was most helpful. Aubrey and I never entertained the thought of me going back out to work. Being at home with our baby was the most important job I would ever undertake and one with the least experience. Hence, learning and budgeting was challenging. I never considered it a sacrifice, but a choice.

We never thought we could be happier. Then three years later, the birth of our second daughter, Tazra, proved us wrong. The joy of holding my babies close to my heart helped me relate more to my mother and the heartache I must have put her through; justifiable or not.

Going without never bothered us; maybe we were too happy to realise how poor we were. Our babies were well looked after and our meals were basic but healthy. Aubrey was forever surprised at my culinary innovations – yes, after four years – and never failed to compliment my effort. However that skill did not extend to his lunches as a student, which for years, was a sandwich and an apple.

One Christmas, my nephew Khal was given a frozen turkey, which he passed on to me. I remembered looking at this huge bird on my kitchen counter and decided that rather than roasting it, I would saw it up; this way I would get many more meals. I called our friend Bert, who had an electric saw and dear Herbie did just that. I eventually made turkey pies, soups and stews. After that we had no appetite for turkey for a very long time.

I always refused money from my parents; I didn't want them to ever think Aubrey was not capable of taking care of his family. The decision we made about him being a full-time student was our choice and we didn't expect help from my parents or anyone else. To ease their concern, I once told them Aubrey had a job after school. I don't think they bought that fib because it never stopped my clever mother from time to time, stocking up our larder with claims that the items were on sale. Little did Ma know, I was aware of all the sales; I had to be, just to get by. I let her have her way, especially when buying for our babies. Unknown to me, she or Pa would put money into my handbag; they ignored my protests and always found some way of giving.

SIXTEEN

Aubrey adjusted well to fatherhood. I recall the moments when his love and consideration never failed to amaze me. When our girls were babies and woke up for their 2am bottle, he always got up, warmed the formula while I changed their diaper and would then lie on the sofa while I fed and burped the baby, sometimes falling asleep there.

Many nights he studied until late and I would insist he remain in bed, but of course he never did. I would try to get up quietly, but being a light sleeper, Aubrey always woke up. Aliya started teething when she was two and a half months old; you could well imagine the sleepless nights for her and us. I recall him pacing the floor with her in his arms and singing one song consistently, "My Bonnie lies over the Ocean", ending it with "Oh bring back my Bonnie to me, to me." I remember thinking in my tired and sleepy state, while taking a break from my bawling baby, "Just one 'to me' love, just one 'to me', at the end of the song."

With insufficient money, two babies and studies, our social life was non-existent. So when Aubrey's sister Maisie and her fiancé were having a party to celebrate their engagement, I insisted he attend the event. Aubrey was reluctant to go because Tazra was only a week old and I was still uncomfortable after a caesarean section. I eventually convinced him to go. When I thought he was at the party, my dear husband drove all the way downtown to our favourite restaurant – which we frequented prior to school days – and brought me a well-dressed lobster. He made sure our babies were settled, placed

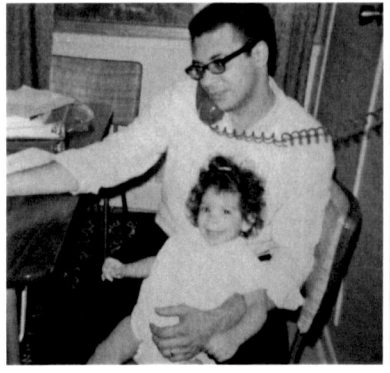 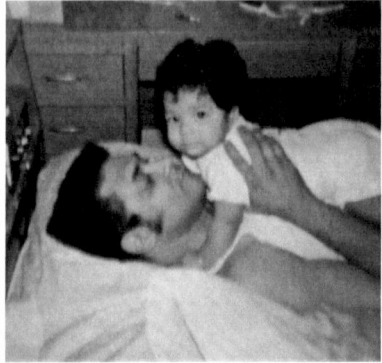

Aliya, 1972, left, and Tazra, 1975

my dinner and me in front of the television set, then went to the party for a couple of hours. I never asked how he paid for that meal!

Aubrey's love and thoughtfulness went beyond that. His youngest sister, Laureen, who worked with a travel agency, obtained five last-minute 'sell off seats' to Barbados for a week of enjoyment in the sun. She offered them to Mater, Zorena, my nephew, Fermin, Aliya and myself. It took quite a bit of persuasion from Aubrey for me to go on that trip. His rationale was, we will make up for the expenditure with his last summer job pay check. But more so, I was going to leave baby Tazra with my mother for the days Aubrey attended school. He prepared a schedule to assure me that both the baby and school would be taken care of with help from Ma. It so happened he decided to do everything himself after Tazra spent the first night sleepless at my parents'. Aubrey then brought her home, where she happily settled in her familiar surroundings and crib. He refrained from telling me this until I returned.

I had prepared and frozen a few dinners for him. His buddies brought home his assignments and also helped with Tazra while he completed his work. I can only imagine the chaos with three young men juggling studies and babysitting. For the longest time the guys referred to Tazra as "our baby girl." After a week of relaxation, to my utter amazement, I returned home to a clean apartment, Tazra and her crib evicted from our bedroom and relocated in Aliya's room, and a pot of Aubrey's famous soup – the only dish he was capable of preparing. But what I especially remember, was one winter morning, I saw him off to school as usual. A few hours later he called and asked me to meet him downtown that afternoon. Prior to calling me, he arranged with his mother to babysit. I met him and we went for an inexpensive meal, then walked down Yonge Street in the cold, holding hands, being content and happy. My dessert was a caramelised apple, bought from the street vendor.

Later while chatting in bed, wondering if I missed some special date in our lives, I asked the reason for our impromptu meal and stroll and he jokingly replied, "Don't you know? This!" As he reached for me. He eventually explained, when we said goodbye that morning I was not my usual chirpy self and he wanted to cheer me up. It's incredible how sometimes the little pleasures in life are the most treasured.

We often did silly things to brighten each other's day. During his years in school I used to write little notes and place them in his lunch bag; funny, romantic, naughty, anything to put a glow in his heart or a smile on his face and make his daily sandwich and apple more appetising. For about a week I neglected to do so, and one morning I found a folded piece of paper under my teacup on which was written: "Our love seems to have taken a vacation, I miss my notes. And Nastyface, thanks for all that you write and mean." That was the first and only time Aubrey acknowledged seeing or reading my notes. After that I made sure, no vacation or neglect.

For years, my notes were faithfully written. I believe they were also sealed in the capsule; he would not have discarded them. I kept the one he left under my teacup! Those student years were tough financially, though there were times when our happiness overshadowed the deprivation. However, we were eagerly anticipating the completion of Aubrey's final year.

Early December, just prior to graduating in the spring, he had a job interview. Aubrey had sent out dozens of applications.

Graduation, 1976

The one we were interested in seemed a promising and interesting job with good benefits, located in a small town in Ontario, close to a lake and ideal for bringing up a young family. He came home after the interview feeling elated, he was confident the job was his. Sharing his excitement, I insisted on hearing everything verbatim. Then two days before Christmas, he was informed that he didn't get the job. That was a rough Christmas; to graduate with no job was not good pre-holiday news.

We then questioned our decision of giving up a job to return to school. At that time, some of our relatives thought it unwise. Were they right? We had saved enough money for a down payment on a house, but it was our dream for Aubrey to obtain a career of his choice instead. For the kids we tried to have a happy Christmas, but for Aubrey and I the New Year seemed dismal. Now back to the drawing board, making sure his one suit and shirt were ready for the next interview in the new year.

Philips Cable and Bell Canada were interviewing on campus and Philips offered him a job. I suggested he also go to Bell, but Aubrey didn't want to be bothered. He was happy with the Philips offer but after some further persuasion from me, he agreed. When he received Bell's reply, he ran up eight flights of stairs to show me the letter. They offered him six hundred dollars more a month; way above the salary scale. Aubrey accepted their offer, then two years later, he was on his way to Saudi Arabia.

In the years ahead, whenever we were disappointed over anything, we remembered Christmas of 1976 and faced our setback with the expectation that it was for the best and better will follow.

SEVENTEEN

Aubrey went on to work with Bell Canada in their downtown office and life seemed to be moving in the right direction for us. We started to pay off his student loan and also save for a down payment on our first house.

After four years of surviving on limited funds, we could now afford dining out sometimes. One birthday we were going out to dinner and a few doors from the restaurant was a boutique with a fur coat in the window. Aubrey suggested we go inside and look around. He ended up buying me a fox and leather jacket. As the sales lady was wrapping it, she asked if it was my birthday, I replied "No, it's his." Many years after that, regardless of my protests, we exchanged presents on his birthday.

Aubrey was employed with Bell Canada for two years when they procured a ten-year contract with the Saudi Arabian Government to update their telecommunications system. Bell provided the Operations and Management training. Two European companies, Ericsson (Sweden) and Philips Telecom (Dutch) joined; they supplied and installed the equipment. The two European companies were referred to as "Joint Venture" by Saudi Telecom.

We were both interested in the idea of living abroad for a few years, especially in a country so geographically and culturally remote. I went to the library and read everything I could about the Kingdom of Saudi Arabia. The more knowledge we acquired, the more intrigued and eager to follow up. We seriously considered the opportunity of living and working in this mysterious land. Both relatives and friends thought us crazy for wanting to move so far from home with two small children. We appreciated their concern but the adventure was too tempting. After much consideration, we decided to venture out. Thank God both of us were on the same page with this. Quite a few families had difficulty adjusting to life in Saudi Arabia. A few marriages broke up and some families left after only a couple of years. One had to stay focused and not worry about the differences in culture, but try to adapt to the entire lifestyle.

In August 1978 Aubrey was off to Riyadh, with the hope that if all goes well, we would join him later. While I was packing his suitcase on the eve of his departure, Aubrey was busy with last minute errands. He came in and handed me an envelope which contained tickets for the girls and I to fly out to California the following day as he. All four of us were sad about the impending separation, so he decided to surprise us with a trip to California, as a distraction. He also made sure we departed prior to him. The thought of us seeing him off would have been too sad for the girls. Needless to say, how we rushed to prepare for the kids and I to leave the next day. We all left for the airport together, Aubrey saw us off and then went on to board his flight to Riyadh via London.

California with my eldest brother and sister-in-law Zed and Lyla was as Aubrey intended, a distraction. He spoke with us from London and the kids were excited to hear his voice, even though they had seen him the previous day. I kept a bright and cheerful disposition for our babies' sake, but my thoughts were with Aubrey, and the hope that we had made the right decision. Tazra, our youngest, was three years old and she missed her father terribly. Disneyland and her two cousins (my niece's children) were not a big enough distraction. Lyla or I always rocked her to sleep and many nights she woke up wanting her Daddy. Aliya was six and understood a bit more why her dad was not there, but was nevertheless sad. I devoted every hour to compensate for the absence of their father. Lyla and Zed pampered them with lots of love, toys and goodies. Our stay was good and would have been perfect had Aubrey been there. Future trips to California were most enjoyable because we always went as a family.

The girls and I returned to Toronto at the end of August, just in time for school, which Aliya attended for three months. Then on December 9th, we left for England until we could join Aubrey.

His first letter from Riyadh.

*****

August 23/1978

My dearest Merle

Here I am in Saudi, from the little I have seen, it is a very strange and fascinating place. I do not think it is possible to completely prepare oneself physiologically for life here. All the stories you have read and heard are true. I am not complaining, only stating facts as I see them. The few Saudis I've met are kind and courteous. This is the month of Ramadan and you cannot imagine how deserted the streets are between the hours of 12 noon – 6pm.

The hotel is comfortable, life here is not one of luxury but I sort of expected that. My first day I think was and I'm sure will be my worst. It was the only time I questioned my decision to come, most of it was the result of being tired and jet lag. Anyhow, I was able to shake off those feelings. I'm referring to a great sense of loss and above all, I really miss you and the kids. Let me assure you, I am well mentally and physically, so don't worry. My job is interesting and will provide me the opportunity to grow with it as the operation expands.

While in London Arif and I discussed and agreed with the way plans are regarding you and the girls going there, so look into it asap.

Once again, I am alright, I know you are worrying, please don't. Will see you guys in London in a couple of months. How are the kids? I enjoyed listening to the tapes you sent from California. Write soon and take care of yourself and our kids. I miss you all. Please tell everyone I am well.

My love always to you and our girls.
Brey

I must have written asking him exactly what his job entailed, this was his reply.

* * * * *

Riyadh,
September 4/1978

My dearest Merle,

The situation is not too bad here. As I have mentioned before, the hardest part of being here is not having you guys with me. It's just as well, why do I say this? The task we are faced with is rather big. We are attempting to do a ten-man job with two persons. This year will be hectic but not as demanding as next year promises to be. After the end of next year, the fun of actually managing the network begins. To give you an idea of the magnitude of the task, we have to set up all records from scratch, provide routines and at the same time implement systems and circuits. The size of the network compares with that of Ontario Region. I also have to prepare a long-range view of the department. It will consist of a complete breakdown of responsibilities and job descriptions, also future manpower requirements. It looks as though we will be here for the remaining decade. Apart from all of

Dhahran, Saudi Arabia

that, the job promises to be interesting and challenging. My part in this is to set up all records and manage the entire intertoll network. Wish me luck! We are presently in a hotel because of a lack of permanent housing. I don't mind the setup because I have made a few friends.

So much about me, how are you and the kids making out? Kiss them for me and tell them I love them very much. Love you, and remember I will see you in London in 107 days. Please send me some photographs of you and the girls.

Semper fidelis,
Brey

After about six weeks in Saudi Arabia, Aubrey went on his first business trip within the Kingdom and I received this letter.

*****

October 6/1978

My dearest Merle,

By now you would have received two tapes and three rolls of film. I have just returned from Jeddah, where I had a most interesting and enjoyable stay. It was enjoyable from the point that it was a change from the hotel and food in Riyadh. Mind you, conditions in Riyadh are not too bad. But the hotel in Jeddah was overlooking a lovely green area. I visited the Red Sea and along the highways one could be disillusioned into believing you are driving in Europe or North America. While in Jeddah, I thought about my R&R in April-May, we should look at Athens or Egypt, discuss this with Laureen or some other country you prefer to visit. I leave the choice of country to you.

Another thing, on our way back to Toronto next July, would you like to go via India and the East to California? I'll have five weeks holiday, so I was thinking we could use that time to fulfil some of your dreams of travelling. Have Laureen give you some info on world tours, also Mediterranean cruises. And all quotes, first class. Anyhow get all the information and take it to England and we'll discuss it.

I listened to the tapes you sent and enjoyed every minute of it. It was great to hear the kids and you, just what I needed after returning from Jeddah. I do not think I can put into words how much I miss you and our girls. Whenever I hear their voices, it tears at my heart and when I hear your voice or read your letters, I miss holding you. I sure miss making love to you, I miss teasing you. Yes, I miss all those things. Many nights I sit and remember giving the girls a piggyback or chair ride, I miss giving Tazi her bottle, I miss waking up during the night and caressing your breasts or bum. But what are the alternatives, I am here to give you and our kids a break in life.

    Merle, I have always wanted the best for you three. I want to buy you lovely things. Sure you usually say, that is not important, maybe it is not but I want them for you anyway, I want little for myself, for you and the kids, everything. There have been times in the past, when I observed folks we know doing things which we would have enjoyed, like travelling or dining out but couldn't afford. I guess I'm tired of feeling the edges of the coin before spending it. I want to assure you and the kids' future. I have not changed my views; all I am doing is expressing how I have always felt. We sacrificed so I could get a career, with the hope of a better future in mind. This being apart is for a short period and one thing I ask, try to explain to the kids and do not let them forget me. Remember, trust in the great maker as you have done in the past and everything will be alright.

    Strange, how the little things are important, I miss our chats over a cup of tea at the kitchen table, I miss watching you dress, I miss running my hand down your tummy ——————— and most of all, I miss ——————— you. I could go on forever but I guess I must stop, for there is nothing I can do now, all I can make are promises of what is in store for you in December. You should book us into a hotel in London for the first couple of nights and also a room for the kids with an adjoining door.

    There is not much more to say, take care of yourself and our kids and remember I love you all very much.

Yours always,
Brey

EIGHTEEN

September to November 1978 was a terribly busy period for me. We were going to England on December 9th until the summer of 1979. Within that time we would see Aubrey in December and April and in the summer he would accompany us to Riyadh.

I had to give up our apartment, store some items and get rid of everything else including our car, all within three months. My biggest worry was the children, with the hope that they adjust well in England. I need not have been concerned, my brother Arif and his family welcomed us with open arms and lots of love, they made our stay most bearable without Aubrey.

Arif spent a lot of time with the girls, he knew how much they missed their Dad and tried to compensate. They remember the enjoyable picnics with their Aunty Pam on the River Lea and how they introduced her to peanut butter and jelly sandwiches, and all the goodies Aunty Ella bought them every Saturday morning when she went shopping.

My nieces and nephews, being older, spent many hours entertaining their little cousins. Those loved ones in England would always occupy a special place in my heart. Aubrey came during the Christmas holidays. We had a fantastic time and the girls and I were over the moon with joy. He left on Boxing Day. The kids and I had settled in nicely and were enjoying England, Arif and his family.

In the summer of 1979, Arif launched his book *West Indians in Britain* which was held at the Dorchester Hotel in London.

It was my first exposure to an event of this magnitude. We the family and some of his staff worked hard with invitations, seating arrangements for dignitaries, loyal supporters, friends and family. The dinner, launching of the book, awards and acknowledgement to folks who contributed to the welfare of West Indians in Britain was successful. A gala to remember! I was very proud of my brother's achievements. My regret was Aubrey couldn't be there for the event.

England was beautiful and expensive. Every month Aubrey transferred a very generous amount of money for me which I spent freely. I remember feeling a bit guilty, for here I was enjoying England, while he was working hard in the desert. I decided to start watching the pennies and slow down on the spending. Also, he knew that going to Greece was at the top of my travel list. From very young, I yearned to travel far and wide. Aubrey was aware of this and I thanked him for making it possible.

This was his reply to my commitment to spending less money.

* * * * *

January 26/1979

My dearest Merle,

I received your letter on the 23rd Jan. and feel I must correct you on a couple of things you mentioned. First of all, you do not have to account to me for the way you are spending the money, nor do you have to promise to conserve it. If after all these years I cannot trust your judgement, then all the things I have been writing you about does not make any sense. Surely, if I trust you with my love, then I can most certainly trust you with money. Besides it's our money, yours, mine and the kids, so my dear, you do not have to make excuses and promises. However you choose to spend it is fine with me.

As regards being thankful for going to Greece, I feel I should be the one to be thankful. You are very much a part of whatever success I achieve. For the days and nights you endured in silence while I was in school, you deserve some recognition. This is a joint venture and any benefits derived, will be shared by all. I remember the sacrifice and denial throughout the years of struggle, your unwavering devotion and support, you should feel entitled to whatever fruits' reaped. So do not stand on the outside of what is happening and express gratitude, continue to be a part of it and take what is rightfully yours. What would I do with the money anyway? I would spend it on things for you.

I want this to be a vacation we will both remember. Book us into the Hilton for four days, (remember a two-bedroom suite or two rooms with an adjoining door), then we could depart for Crete and Rhodes. Incidentally, you could travel BA560 leaving London 9:35 arriving Athens 15:00.

You stated in our phone conversation on Sunday that you received my last letter and enjoyed reading it. I wonder if it is because of the risqué talk. Anyhow whether or not you believed what I wrote, I was sincere when I made those statements, I would say those things to only you. Excuse this muddle, I am a bit tired, although I am tired I would not refuse a little bit of you right now.

I cannot tell you how much I am looking forward to Greece, as I have said before, come prepared, any and everything goes, I have quite a few plans for you. Right now, if you were here I would ——————. Now, now, don't get too excited as yet Babe, let's wait until Greece. **I PROMISE, YOU WILL REMEMBER GREECE!**

Say hello to everyone. Oh! I almost forgot, how are our kids? Kiss them for me. So long love, take care of yourself and the kids and remember, I love you three very much.

Love, Brey

Whenever my letters to him were melancholy, his replies always lifted my spirits. His words were consoling without making me feel awful or ungrateful for the life I lived ... but how I missed him!

* * * * *

February 2/1979

My dearest Merle

Just came in from work and decided to write you a few lines. I was reflecting on the two events of my life that have had a pronounced effect.

a) Marrying you

b) Returning to school

I feel marrying you provided me with the incentive to be successful in life. And returning to school was a manifestation of that incentive. We do not have anything to be discontented about. We are both healthy and love each other very much, the same goes for the kids. Also, we are on the threshold of fulfilling our dreams. This sacrifice we are presently going through, is of our own choosing, but one I am sure, which will enrich our lives in more ways than one. It is a good feeling to find out I do love you just as much, or more, as when I first met you. I thank God this parting is temporary. And remember, none of this would have been possible if we did not get married.

Have you ever wondered what paths our lives would have taken, separately? That thought I cannot ponder. I do love you very much and when I say I love you, I mean I love you for who you are, I love you for what you have made of me, I love the way we need each other and yes, I do love and enjoy you physically.

No, I'm not becoming old and sentimental, it is just that today I asked myself, why am I working so hard? And the only answer I could arrive at was, for my family. For my wife because she deserves the best, for my children because I want them to have the best. It is purely for you three. So, you see darling, let us endure this temporary separation and before you know it, we'll be together as a family soon.

So much for that, now let us turn to my favourite topic, yes, I know yours too. Tell me, do you dream of the pleasures we will indulge in while in Greece? Well I do, some things, should I mention, will make you blush, like ————————. Remember, this is my fantasy, you must come up with your own. Give me a hint in your next letter. Let your hair down, no shyness now, after all we have known each other for a lifetime, just write what is on your mind as well as in your heart. I expect a direct reply to this letter.

Anyhow my love, with that I must say so long until I hear from you. Tell the kids I love and miss them very much. As for you my darling Nastyface, there is no need to say, "I love you," by now you should know it!

Love, Brey

I wish he had not sealed away my letters; I recall only some of my replies.

* * * * *

Riyadh, February 17/1979

My dearest Merle,

I received your letter with the photographs, the kids look so lovely, a tribute to Mom. Nothing new is happening on this side of the fence. The weather is amazingly comfortable to date.

In your last letter, you stated you were feeling a bit guilty about holidaying in England while I was working in Riyadh. Please do not feel that way, enjoy England as much as possible. We both have our jobs to do. You make this a memorable experience for our girls. This way the impact of my not being there will be lessened. When you were going through the pain and discomfort during pregnancy and childbirth, I got off relatively free. Now you and the kids have a good time. Enjoy England, Arif and the family. All that I ask, don't let them forget me, after all Taz was only three when I left. Aliya and I talk, she is indeed our little lady. Please write and let me know everything they say and do. How I miss them.

Sorry I missed your birthday, seeing I was not there, let me describe what I was thinking. So here goes, you guessed right, your delayed present from me ——————. I owe you that among many others. My dearest, I cannot tell you how much I love and miss you guys. I love each of you differently, you it is a love mixed with a dependency, with the kids, it is a love combined with a need to protect. Take care of yourself and our girls.

Kisses for the kids and regards to all in England.
Love, Brey

* * * * *

February 21/1979

My dearest Merle,

I had a few minutes, so I decided to write my favourite girl. I do not have anything concrete to write about, so I will just ramble on and try to stay away from telling you about the mischief you and I could get into if you were here.

The project is progressing nicely and there is a possibility it will be expanded by 50%. I don't know what this means for Bell. There are rumours that they are bidding on a contract in China, no details are available. I am still working long hours and am enjoying the best of health, Dick was quite ill of late and has lost 15 pounds, he's ok now.

As I have said before, this being apart is hard, but nonetheless, there are some positive things about it. For one, I am convinced that I love you and always will, I have also come to realise how much you and the kids mean to me. Every time this place gets me down, I think about you three and this fills me with required energy to keep on going. There is so much I want for you guys, mostly I want to assure your future, I don't want us struggling when we are older, I want to have the money for the kids' university. Sure, I have always said money is not important, that is only true if you have it.

Another thing I have come to realise and that is – life would be unbearable without you and the kids. You see a man must have people to love and he must also have a purpose in life. You guys are my love and purpose. We do not have anything to be ungrateful about. Life has been relatively good to us, the past has not been bad, and the future promises to be better. So, my love have faith. Right now, I would like to be telling you these things in person. Anyhow, there is still a lot of time left, I will get my opportunity.

Received your last letter, yes, the wicked one and enjoyed it. Hope you'll honour those promises. Trust me, I'll hold you to it.

Take care of yourself and our kids, always remember I do love you.

Love, Brey

I remember that naughty letter; just as well it's sealed away. It would have placed this book under a different category.

*****

February 24/1979

My dearest Merle,

Just a few lines to let you know I am thinking of you guys. I cannot remember when, if ever, I have thought of anyone or anything, as often as I think of you and our kids. You three occupy every spare moment of my thoughts. The kids occupy my thoughts during the day, thoughts of you are reserved for my more intimate moments. During the day everything is alright but at night the need for companionship becomes difficult to suppress. I guess the daytimes are not too bad, because even in Toronto, I was away from home all day. I combat some of the loneliness by working long hours. I have had a lot of time to do some personality analysis and you would be surprised to know I have found out a few things about myself which, I too am surprised to discover. Those undesirable things, yes, my impatience, quick temper etc. I am trying to change, you must admit my temper evaporates just as quickly.

Hope you realise how much I love you and the extent to which I am going, to prove it. I say this with all sincerity, I do love you and always will, I say it with more maturity. It is also more meaningful, those years prior to our marriage I said I loved you, in those days it had a different meaning, today I say it with more commitment. What I am trying to say is that I love you more now, than I did then. This is a good thing to find out after twelve years of marriage. It is also good to be able to say that my wife is the best person I know. And it's a pleasure to know that after twelve years, we still need and want each other. I so miss not having you to cuddle, there are times when I feel that need to kiss you tenderly. And we are so compatible most times, when you are not aggravating me but most of all, how we enjoy each other.

Anyhow, as much as I would like to continue writing, I must close. Take care of yourself and the girls.

Always remember how much I love and miss you three.
Love, Brey

The day after Aubrey wrote the letter above, he called and was not a bit interested in discussing our finances. I was rambling on and didn't listen or answer any of his questions.

That very day he wrote the following.

* * * * *

February 25/1979

My Sweet Confusion,

I am a bit put out with myself for becoming impatient with you. It is not you but me. If I sounded a bit irritated, I am sorry! As I have said in my last letter, I am trying to overcome my impatience. I hope to curb it before I leave this place. Darling, whenever I phone, please do not try to tell me about unimportant things, e.g. bank, hotel accommodation etc. The time is too short and I would rather use it to discuss you and the kids, write to me about anything else. Items of that nature, as far as I am concerned, it is not that important that it cannot be handled by mail. All I would like to hear about when I call, is how you and the kids are doing and if you have any problems, anything else is secondary. I hate myself for getting angry with you, you do not deserve it. Go ahead and sort out the money situation with the bank, you could send some to the other account and you decide on the hotel and make the reservation. I trust your judgement. Surely, by now you must realise you do not need my approval to do anything, I am confident you are capable. The only stipulation regarding the hotel, reserve a two-bedroom suite, with a queen size bed or two rooms with an adjoining door. As usual, it is always a pleasure speaking with you guys. I do love you very much you know, yes, even if you are a bit of an irritation at times.

Take care my love, and kiss our kids for me.
Love, Brey

NINETEEN

I must have written when I was missing Aubrey and feeling a bit down. I also told him to stay away from all those expat ladies in the Kingdom. This was his reply of assurance and fidelity.

* * * * *

March 5/1979

My dearest Merle,

It is about fifty-two days before I see you guys, then two weeks of fun and laughter.

Your letter had an 'unMerle' tone, that is, it did not sound like my girl who endured so many years of sacrifice. I guess your reaction is natural, being apart is no fun but remember, there are a lot of positive things that will happen because of us being away from each other. I too sometimes question the validity of it all. My love, this separation is temporary but the results will be so beneficial. I know it's hard but nothing is achieved without sacrifice. I also know you must have been going through a rough patch when that letter was written, you sounded better on the phone. Keep the faith my love and remember, we'll be together soon.

I believe Bell is trying to obtain contracts in Mexico and Brazil and is negotiating another one in China. I guess they are trying to set up internationally. The work here is overwhelming, we are only scratching the surface, there is not enough manpower to do the job. Anyhow, we are doing our best.

So much for that, let us discuss the more important things in life. I was very pleased to hear the voices of my beloved ones. I, like you, do miss our times together and so long to just be with you, I also miss having those little ones sit on my knees and compete for my attention. How I would like to comfort Tazra whenever she is hurt and listen to Aliya as she discovers the joys of life. To sum it up, I miss my family very much but I still have time to enjoy them. I have no doubt that we will benefit positively from this experience.

Incidentally, please try your best to send Aliya to horseback riding lessons, during our conversation last Sunday she stated that she would like to go. I am so pleased that you guys are comfortable and happy with Arif and the family.

Rest assured, you will not have to resort to violence to prevent me looking at other women, I have no desire to do so. As the saying goes, "when a man has steak at home, why would he want to go out for hamburger?" So dear, do not worry about that ever happening. You have a lot going for you, I love you, you are a good wife and mother. Apart from that, we make good music together. All in all, you are a winner!!

With those lines I will close. So, take care of yourself and our kids and remember, I love you very much.

Love, Brey

Thirty-five days before Athens.

* * * * *

My dearest Merle,

Just a few lines to let you guys know I am still alive and thinking of you. Do you realise it is only 35 days to Athens? Received your two letters and as usual enjoyed reading them. I know the frequency with which I have been writing has decreased. I want to complete a couple of projects prior to going on vacation. You cannot imagine how much I'm looking forward to seeing you three. The girls sounded so grown up on the phone. How I long to hold them and listen to their stories and joys at discovering life. I imagine Tazra trying to explain something and so excited about it, that she stutters. It is kind of scary, Aliya is seven, in a few years she will be all grown up. How is she adjusting in school and how is terror Tazra making out, does she still sulk when she doesn't get her way? I hate that thought when they must leave us. When we are no longer needed. Anyhow, that's life and my love, long after they have left home, we will still have each other.

Dear Merle, you really do not realise how much I love you. I never thought it was possible to love someone so much. As for our kids I love them in an entirely different way. A more protective and nurturing way. As I've mentioned before, this was supposed to be a few lines, one not completed without my saying again, l love you!

Love, Brey

Greece, timeless Greece! History, Archaeology, sunshine, blue seas and most of all, my love is here. We are home! Home to Aubrey and I, is when the four of us are together. He flew in from Riyadh, the girls and I from London. We were supposed to meet at the airport but missed each other and I eventually took a taxi to the hotel. Upon arrival, I held out a few bills to the driver and he took what I thought was reasonable. Out of somewhere a policeman appeared, took back quite a few drachmas and returned them to me. The driver had a sheepish look; I smiled, for nothing could have irritated me that day. I collected our luggage and checked in. After taking care of the girls, I went for a shower. Aubrey arrived while I was still there and joined me. When I mentioned the kids, he said not to worry, the toys he brought would keep them occupied. I could not contain myself; running ten kilometres would not have made my heart beat any faster.

Greece lived up to our expectations. Both Aubrey and I are interested in archaeology, history and mythology and all of that oozed out of every grain of sand and dirt. The girls were just as excited, and we took the time to explain everything in detail. They too got hooked, especially Aliya, her questions were endless. Tazra was mostly interested in picking the poppies.

While visiting a church Aliya asked her dad the age and he told her, 11th century AD. "That's new, I want to see the BC things, Dad." How they enjoyed us being together as a family. Aubrey loved, played and spoilt them. We devoted a few hours to them every day, doing the things kids enjoy; a visit to the zoo, playing in the park with the local children, eating all the fun foods and buying souvenirs and toys.

Bedtime stories were discussing the mythological characters and their tales, Aliya's favourite was Pan. Tazra was content to sit on her father's lap while he read. We also told them the legend of Helen of Troy and how it was portrayed during a festival in Guyana, and that was when their dad and I met. Years later while holidaying in Turkey, we visited the remains of Troy.

Daytime was occupied with the kids and touring Greece. The evenings belonged to us. Long, glorious nights. We talked, ate, made love and slept, waking at intervals only to start all over again. Lovemaking with Aubrey was not just a heated and physical gratification. Our souls mingled, emotions shredded, tears flowed and that feeling of excitement, commitment and deep reverence spread throughout my body. Agreeing with Joseph Addison: *"Love is a second life; it grows into the soul, warms every vein and beats in every pulse."*

After a glimpse of heaven we were leaving; Aubrey returning to Riyadh, the girls and I to London. Aliya clung to her dad and cried. Tazra, only four years old, held on to me, looked wide-eyed and totally unhappy. If I occupied Aubrey's heart, then Aliya and Tazra had his soul. He seemed so sad, my heart broke for him. I at least had the girls and was returning to my brother and his family, but Aubrey was returning to a strange land, work and no family. My one consolation was, this will be our last parting. Many years later, as a Father's Day gift, the girls compiled an album with photographs taken in some of the countries we visited. They composed the following and attached it to the album.

Travels with My Father

Once upon a time a young man and his family embarked on a series of journeys. They visited far away places littered with sacred sites and ruins. They wandered through historical churches and mosques. They touched archaeological structures bleached by the sun. Knowing his daughters were young and easily exhausted, he sandwiched ice cream cones and visits to the zoo between the art galleries and museums. What the young man didn't know was, that these trips moulded and changed the lives of his daughters. You see, although they were young, they were impressionable and these trips became part of who they are. One travels for experience and enlightenment. A child who travels will grow up never forgetting the diversity and vastness of the world. And the young man, who himself has now grown, should never forget the importance of the experiences he has given to his daughters.

TWENTY

It was now time for us to join Aubrey in Saudi Arabia. There was so much to be done. Pack, return to Toronto, unpack, repack, vaccinations, place household items which I had bought in England, into storage, and most of all, sad farewells to our family and friends.

* * * * *

May 18/1979

My dearest Wife,

The only thing that spoiled our holiday in Greece was the parting. I felt so helpless at the airport when Aliya started to cry. As a result, I promised myself, I will never do this again. Wherever I go, my family goes. How I love you three. Apart from that, it was an enjoyable holiday. Aliya's reaction at the airport has caused me to make a change of plans. This is what I think we should do.

Concentrate on Aliya finishing the Ontario Board of Education course, even if that means taking her out of school next month and you teaching her. She should complete that course as soon as possible, it is very important for entrance into the International school.

You said you wanted at least three weeks in Canada, then you should arrange to leave England no later than

June 29th. I agree, that does not leave you much time. I intend to arrive in Canada July 13th, we all then leave for London July 17th, then on to Riyadh on the 19th. So, work on these plans. Get your smallpox shots in England, this is important, the series of shots must be spaced over a period of 3-4 weeks. I spoke to the guy who assigns housing and he said not to worry, he'll find us a villa. I will inform the Toronto office so they could start to arrange orientation for you also hotel accommodation.

So love, in less than two months we will be together again as a family. I felt so depressed after seeing how sad you three were at Athens airport. Tell the kids I will be coming to take them to Saudi and promise, we will never part again. Do remember, I love you and always will. See you at 9:15 a.m. on July 13th in Toronto. Please write to Richard and tell him of our plans. I would also like to see Pa and Ma while there. Hello to the old lady, Arif, Pam, Ella and the kids.

So long love,
Brey

P.S. GREECE WAS GOOD!!!

* * * * *

May 22/1979

My dearest Merle,

I have been able to shake that sad and down feeling which I've had since returning from Athens. It is almost two weeks since seeing you guys but the most enjoyable thing about that is, I will see you all in fifty-one days. Attached is a copy of the telex I sent to the Toronto Office, call them upon arrival and they will arrange everything. And remember, you and the kids get your smallpox *vaccination in London, the others cholera, tetanus and polio in Toronto. I have changed my travelling plans and will spend more time in Toronto (two weeks). Will call and tell you the details. Thanks to you and the kids for the lovely cards.*

Anyhow my love, take care of yourself and our kids and always remember how very much I love you.

Love, Brey

Moving to Saudi Arabia presented a whole new chapter in our lives. We arrived in the middle of August, late in the evening. I was dressed appropriately, covered from neck to ankle; during the late seventies and eighties all foreign women were required to wear long dresses or skirts. The temperature was 40-45c, but strangely that didn't bother me much, as everywhere was air-conditioned. And the humidity level was typical of a desert. The company rented a block of villas as temporary accommodation until a compound was built. We occupied a large three-bedroom bungalow fully equipped, with appliances to teaspoons, a chest freezer, patio furniture, and anything else required was supplied by Support Services, a large warehouse that stocked just about everything. Most of the household items and small appliances were bought in both Europe and the United States, therefore the outlets throughout the villas were dual voltage. All that was needed to make it home was our personal touch. Family photographs, little keepsakes, our books and music. They even supplied us with some groceries, a thoughtful act, especially when one has children.

Waking up to silence and a bright room, despite the drawn drapes, I stepped outside. After being taken aback by the blast of heat, glaring sunshine and beautiful cloudless sky, I noticed our entire yard was covered with little rocks. My first thought was, "this is dangerous for the kids." Mentioning my concern to Aubrey, he said it was the only way to contain the sand, especially during a sandstorm. I had forgotten for a moment that we were in the desert.

Our villa was surrounded with a tall wrought iron fence and gate where a profusion of bougainvillea plants grew. Since living in Saudi Arabia, I have learnt to appreciate the bougainvillaea much more; those hearty flowers bloomed under harsh conditions. Many times they enhanced our home with their beauty. Later that day, Aubrey took us for a drive around the city. Riyadh looked like a huge construction site with many cranes on nameless streets. Everything green was missing, except for a few date palms which were covered with sand and dust and looked more brown than green. Looking around and feeling a little disappointed – only because of the tales I read as a child – I thought, where is the wonder and mystery of the 'Arabian Nights?' I was obviously in the wrong country.

Saudi Arabia was on a five-year development plan, with a budget of about 260 billion dollars. Every – mostly European – architect's dream was fully realised. I'm sure they were given a free rein to be creative, with no limit on funds. They constructed beautiful marble structures that gleamed under the sun, and in the evenings on dark streets, the buildings shimmered like the many stars above. Because of the heat, dust and no life form, neither human nor animal, during the daytime, one could experience that feeling of being on foreign and forbidden ground. But in the evening, everything came to life. Construction started up, shops reopened and the souks – markets – bustled with business.

I settled in, happy that we were all together again, despite the inconveniences I encountered, like getting accustomed to wearing full length attire when going out beyond the compound walls. At that time, long skirts, high necks and long sleeves were sufficient, but in the nineties we had to wear abayas just like the Saudi ladies. Abayas, long black robes worn over your clothing, had its advantages, especially the Westernised front zippered version, for who knew what was worn underneath; nothing or anything to keep one cool.

Unavailable were some food items the kids were accustomed to, like peanut butter, ketchup, cereals and fresh milk. There were a couple of supermarkets the size and stock of a convenience store, with basic staples. Very early on, we women learnt to make ketchup, mayonnaise, tomato sauce and other condiments. We kept our flour in the freezer to ward off the weevils. And every night we mixed powdered milk and had to disguise the taste with chocolate powder, which was brought in from Canada, for our children. But then there was an abundance of delicious fresh bread and after a while sliced bread was included. All the kids on the compound were excited because now they could have 'proper' peanut butter and jelly sandwiches.

There were also fruits and vegetables from that part of the world, seafood arrived every morning from the Red Sea. Nuts and spices were in abundance, some of which we had never seen or used before, all available at the souks.

Potable water was trucked in from a desalination plant in Jubail, approximately four hundred kilometres away and purchased from gas stations, where we filled our jerry cans for a nominal fee. The little shops stocked Perrier water which we all bought by the case and every household drank it all day.

Meat, chicken, butter and cheese were imported from Europe. Aubrey and I were especially partial to the butter from Ireland, in my opinion the best I've tasted. Sometime during our years in Riyadh I ate camel and ostrich meat, both too gamey for my palate and I also drank camel's milk, which went down quite well.

In the early eighties when returning from summers in Canada, we all brought huge suitcases filled with food and other items such as greeting cards, gift wrap, candles and specific toys not available in the Kingdom. One Thanksgiving, most of our friends forgot to pack cranberry sauce and my one can was divided between five families. Generosity and camaraderie was a constant bond among us expats.

Once, a Bell Canada official came into the Kingdom and we hosted a reception for him at the clubhouse. He asked the ladies what one food item we would like and the majority shouted "maple syrup". A couple of weeks later, a can of the finest Canadian maple syrup was delivered to each home.

Four years later, supermarket chains, from France and the United States, opened up and stocked international products, some items not available in Canada. Many of us left Saudi Arabia with improved culinary skills. Apart from learning to improvise, having so many international friends and sharing recipes were indeed advantageous.

TWENTY-ONE

Living in the Middle East afforded us a comfortable lifestyle, despite certain restrictions. We ladies were not legally permitted to work, with or without pay, as was stamped in our passports, but we eventually "worked" our way around that decree, all by word of mouth and who was willing to take the risk by employing women. I worked for a company that equipped hospitals with everything from furniture and medical equipment, to cotton swabs and bandages. I was in the Accounting department and dealt in at least five or six currencies. It was a challenging job which I enjoyed immensely. There were days when my boss called to inform me that my driver would not be picking me up. Most companies provided chauffeurs for their female employees.

Every so often, the Ministry of Labour checked offices for female workers and if found, the company would be heavily fined and our spouses would also be held responsible. It was always the husbands' fault when their wives broke the law. I'm sure most ladies would agree, it was a very favourable law.

Being chauffeured back and forth within the confines of the car allowed us to communicate more freely with our drivers. They were just as curious about our lifestyle as we theirs, so conversing was always interesting and amusing. Khalaf, my Saudi driver from the first company I worked for looked too young to be driving, much less chauffeuring and seemed younger still in his attitude. Like most drivers, Khalaf never acknowledged stop signs; this was prior to traffic lights in Riyadh. When I reprimanded him, his rationale was, "Madam, no cars coming from the left, no cars on the right, only someone with no brains would stop." All verbalised in Arabic. I closed my eyes most times and prayed. God must have heard me, for we always arrived safely.

Khalaf's pleasant and amusing attitude made up for his bad driving habits. He always admired a leather jacket I wore – at that time, abayas were not worn by expats – and asked me to bring back one exactly like mine for him, from Canada. I agreed but explained that his may differ, because the male patterns are straight cut and ladies curved at the waist and hips. Khalaf was adamant, claiming, "same, same, or none". I took off mine and gave it to him. He wore it proudly throughout the cold months and beyond.

I could write volumes of anecdotes about Khalaf, and years later Aziz, who chauffeured me while I worked at the King Saud International School. Aziz was from Bangladesh and was a more cautious driver, and subtly curious about Westernised lifestyle. After hearing my phone calls some days to Aubrey, suggesting he bring home some dinner, Aziz once asked me if "Hon" was Aubrey's other name, and quoting him, "Madam, you always call Mr Aubrey, "Hon." Maybe he like me call him Mr Hon, yes?" My reply, upon realising he was serious was, "No, Aziz, I think he would prefer you to continue calling him, Mr Aubrey."

Returning to the Kingdom in the nineties, I worked at the Canadian Embassy and King Saud International School. Now, years later, laws about women working have since changed, and Saudi and expat ladies now have careers and work in various jobs.

Aliya and Tazra adjusted well in The Saudi Arabian International School with students from over fifty countries. We travelled as a family three times a year for eight years, until our girls went on to high school. Yes, life was wonderful!

Our first holiday was spent in Jordan. We especially wanted to visit Petra and the Dead Sea. Being at home in Toronto with our babies afforded me the time to read many books and magazines on cultures and places far and wide. This

Jerash Jordan, 1980

included National Geographic magazines, which we always seemed to have enough money to subscribe to. I once borrowed a book from the library on the Hashemite Kingdom of Jordan and as Aubrey and I mulled over the chapter covering Petra, we were amazed and impressed. After reading about this sandstone city, we hoped one day to visit Jordan. And it so happened, years later living in Saudi Arabia afforded us the opportunity. By the time we had repatriated and because Aubrey and I were interested in archaeology and ancient history, my brain was saturated with the Greeks, Romans, Prophets, Pharaohs, Gods, Bedouins and Nabataeans. Holidaying in Jordan was one of my most memorable, maybe because it was so culturally different from Europe or the Far East.

Eventually and with much anticipation, we were on a flight to, at last, Jordan! On the first day after our arrival in Amman, we rented a car and headed out to the Dead Sea, which was approximately sixty-five kilometres from the capital. We told the girls about the Dead Sea being a lake and also the lowest point on Earth. We also explained that because of its salt content, no fish or plants could survive and we would float and not try to swim, because our eyes would burn if water gets into them. They were impressed and couldn't wait to get into the water, especially after seeing a few older folks reading while floating in a reclining position. Apparently, because the water contained so many minerals, it was beneficial to curing some ailments and lots of seniors frequented it.

I warned our girls not to put their heads under water. I had forgotten, children will do exactly what you forbid. Tazra dunked and came up crying, and Aliya complained about her skin burning; they were 5 and 8 years old. We immediately washed them off with all but one bottle of the drinking water we brought from the hotel. Thank goodness the concierge had insisted we take lots of water. Once dry and anointed with some soothing oil, they happily walked along the beach with their father admiring a few camels, while I went into the water again. It was a most astounding experience; I floated in various positions, lying on my back, reclining with my arms and legs pointing up to the sky. By then the others had left, so I had the entire area to myself while I did my antics, confident that no one saw me. Much to my pleasure, those were the days when the Dead Sea on the Jordanian side was hardly frequented. There were no restaurants, hotels, change rooms or showers. Now, over forty years later, I believe all are available.

The following day after loading up the car with a picnic lunch and again, lots of drinking water, we headed out to Petra. This took us longer than the approximate three hours, because we went via the King's Highway, which happened to be the older and more scenic route. During our leisurely drive and way off the highway, we saw many Bedouins, some dressed in striped thobes on their camels and other shepherds tending to their goats and sheep. It was just like a biblical movie setting, and we would not have been surprised to see Mr Heston stepping out from amongst the animals, expecting to autograph something for us.

We eventually arrived at the main entrance to the city of Petra and were told we had to go in on horseback, for only the horses could navigate around the huge boulders. We rode in and were accompanied by a young archaeologist who volunteered to show us around for the day. Upon seeing this beautifully carved sandstone city, I marvelled at what the Nabataeans built over three centuries BC. We walked through the carved temples, caves, tombs and the famous treasury in awe. Aubrey went into the tombs, while I remained with the children. We were the only visitors at the time and were told by our guide Niazi – whom we kept in touch with for many years – that Petra was frequented mainly by archaeologists. Now after four decades, it is the main tourist attraction in Jordan.

We sat down to lunch later, which we shared with our new *sadiq*, as he chatted about his days as an archaeological student and the benefits of living close to Petra. Later in the afternoon Niazi left, but not before inviting us to his home for dinner, which we declined but promised to visit for a few minutes. A Bedouin who resided in one of the caves in Petra, had invited us for tea. Living in the Middle East taught us, one does not refuse such hospitality, which is considered an honour.

His abode was cosy and not too hygienic. We shared the space with his two wives, children and goats. They were so warm and friendly, that sitting on the dirt warding off the goats and flies while sipping tea, made one feel privileged to be in their home. We laughed and chatted, mainly with gestures when language became incomprehensible, but our children played together with no problems communicating. I was very proud of our little girls, Aliya drank her tea, a beverage she never acquired a taste for but knew it was impolite to refuse. Prior to entering the cave, I warned Tazra – who enjoyed tea, made the Arabic way, black and sweet – to sip her tea slowly, because her glass would be refilled continuously. I did not tell her I was concerned about the water not being boiled long enough. My little five year old imp, disregarded my darting looks and kept on enjoying many glasses of her favourite drink. My fears were unwarranted, she never had any after effects.

After a most enjoyable time spent in their company, we bade farewell to our host and his wives, whose faces were covered the duration of our visit. They were truly hospitable and their children beautiful. We rode out of Petra after a most interesting visit. We then drove to Niazi's home situated in Wadi Musa, another place steeped in history, where we revisited a few days later. We met his parents and siblings who were warm and friendly. They invited us to stay for a meal, but we graciously refused because of the time and distance back to the hotel.

After a long day of ancient history, new friendships and heat, we started back to our hotel at sunset. By the time we arrived in Amman, it was dark, the girls asleep in the back and we were lost! Upon departing the hotel that morning, I thought we had our route clearly mapped out. I was the navigator and my directions led us astray. After many detours on nameless streets, we eventually arrived at the capital. That evening it seemed that all the Jordanians living in Amman were out on the streets socialising, arguing, debating, or protesting and the ones we asked for directions spoke no English. Aubrey and I were embarrassed because of our limited knowledge of Arabic. A policeman eventually came to our rescue and led the way on his motorcycle, directly to our hotel entrance. Aliya and Tazra slept through the whole commotion.

TWENTY-TWO

Apart from the annual two R & R's, the girls and I were away in July and August. We spent one month in Canada or England – where Aubrey would meet us – or in some other country for the other month. Prior to leaving, I always prepared, labelled and froze twenty meals for him; maybe this was done mainly to ease my conscience, rather than providing him with a home cooked dinner. After all, restaurants were plentiful in Riyadh. I disliked being away from him, but Riyadh is unbearably hot and arid during the summer. The girls would be indoors too much. Hence, most of us mothers took our children to cooler climes.

During our years in the Kingdom, we tried to expose our girls to different cultures. This was done without much effort because of the travelling. We also befriended a few Saudi families, and most of the workers and their families were expats from around the globe.

Aliya and Tazra grew up with empathy, a good sense of belonging and strong ethical values. The leisurely lifestyle in Riyadh also afforded us the luxury to bond as a family. The men quit work at three thirty, hence there was time for family and activities. The best times were around our dining room table, just us four, where we sat for hours during mealtimes, chatting about everything, from how our day went to some world events. We were careful not to burden them with too much information. Aubrey and I however, always encouraged most topics and from very young Aliya and Tazra voiced their thoughts and opinions, which we respected. Those were golden moments with my family. I would give anything to relive those years.

Like most children living in the Middle East, they were very much aware of the unrest in that part of the world and I believe became better people because of that knowledge. I think we parents underestimate the logic, knowledge and sometimes crafty ways of our children.

One evening, we invited some of the men working in Aubrey's department for dinner. They were in Riyadh without their families and every so often we and other families on the compound had the single guys over for a home cooked meal. As the gentlemen arrived, Aliya and Tazra were outside playing and painting rocks – one of their favourite recreational activities. Unknown to us, they were selling their artistic masterpieces to our guests. The guys left their purchases outside to dry. We did not discover this embarrassing transaction until the following day, when our little entrepreneurs asked to be taken shopping, to spend their profits. The men refused refunds and kept the rocks, so Aubrey ended up treating them to lunch as compensation for being ripped off by two little girls. Have I mentioned our daughters grew up with strong ethical values? I guess that was acquired years later!

Dinner parties were the most frequent form of entertainment. One evening, thirteen of us were around the table discussing our cultures, traditions and politics when we realised eleven of us were from different countries. When we thought it appropriate, our girls were included. We also dined at the many international restaurants, which were segregated between families and single men. Some restaurants were elaborately decorated, others basic. However, regardless of the ambience, the food was always delicious and the portions generous. After dinner, we usually tried walking off some of our newly acquired calories, by going to the souks.

During the seventies to nineties, there were no cinemas or any place for social gatherings apart from each other's home or restaurants. Most of us had friends working at various

Tazra – falcon souk

embassies and were invited to their social events, which was a treat because they served authentic alcohol and not the homemade brew. Being an Islamic country, alcohol is forbidden. A law defied by some daring folks was wine making. A few expats mastered the art and claimed it tasted better than what they made in their country because of the superior quality of grape juices available in the Kingdom.

Apart from entertaining in our homes, we also had backyard potluck dinners with about twelve other families. One such evening, my friend, Cher, presented us with a jar of live cockroaches. I have no idea how she collected them. As after dinner entertainment, she suggested we have a "roach race" and proceeded to draw a large chalk circle on the ground. She had painted different colours on the roaches backs and instructed us all to select a colour and place our bets. She then emptied the contents of the jar in the middle of the circle; my green roach came in first, reaching the perimeter before the others. It must have heard me screaming encouragement, while standing on a chair. The elation of winning 100 riyals (approx. $35) was worth the dread of being near so many roaches. What we lacked in access to entertainment, we made up with innovative and creative ideas to amuse ourselves.

In 1980, our then Prime Minister Pierre Trudeau, came on a state visit to Saudi Arabia. Being the largest Canadian contingent working in the Kingdom, we were honoured with a visit. Mr Trudeau accompanied with a Prince, arrived at our compound escorted by the king's royal guards. The impressive convoy of approximately half a dozen red convertible Mercedes Benz pulled up. The royal guards looked smart in their khaki uniform, accessorised with red berets, lanyards, epaulettes, and belts. Between the convertibles was a black Rolls Royce. Mr Trudeau and His Royal Highness stepped out.

Because we were living on the temporary compound, the tennis courts were the only area large enough to host the event. We waved our Canadian flags and cheered upon seeing him. It was surreal standing there in the heat, greeting our Prime Minister on a tennis court thousands of miles from home. After the usual formalities, Mr Trudeau mingled with us like old friends getting together. Needless to say, we ladies had a better visit with him, while our husbands stepped aside knowing they couldn't compete. Throughout the visit, the Prince smilingly watched on, while chatting with the men.

Bell Canada's compound was completed in 1981. The Administration building, where Aubrey's office was located, and the Data Centre, were just on the other side of the resident wall. Eventually, another impressive building was built for the Minister of Telecommunications and his staff. To get to the residents compound, one had to pass through two sets of guarded gates; first to the office buildings, then residential. Years later, the whole area was dubbed 'Telephone City'.

Our housing consisted of apartment buildings for single guys and couples with one child, and three bedroom townhouses for families with more children. Again it was fully furnished, everything new; we ladies could not have been happier with all the amenities. Also available were swimming pools, tennis courts, a race track, a soccer field, two clubhouses with a recreational manager to organise activities, a medical clinic, a gas pump – our men drove company cars – a restaurant at no cost to the single men, and shopping buses for the ladies. When not shopping, we played bridge, board games, or some other activity three or four times a week.

A weekly communiqué prepared by volunteers was delivered to our villas informing us of all the activities, outings etc. Some families employed a male domestic help – "houseboy" a title I regard as politically incorrect, however commonly used in the Kingdom – to do our cleaning and/or cooking. Television shows were limited to pre-recorded American and British programmes. Saudi Arabia at that time had only two English speaking channels. Then in the nineties, television programmes became International and we saw shows, some live, from Germany, England, Lebanon, Holland, India, Hong Kong, Australia, Pakistan, Egypt, France, and the United States. I especially enjoyed the German Christmas shows and recalled getting hooked on the French soap opera Riviera'. We were comfortable in our little corner in the desert. Life was cool for all... especially us ladies!

TWENTY-THREE

We did most of our shopping at the souks. A most enlightening experience. When I think of the souks, I see a large market with some sort of chaotic order. Upon entering the area, your senses were heightened by the smell of food, frankincense burning, spices, sometimes sewerage and many unrecognisable scents.

Everything was organised into sections and exposed to the dust and odour. The vendors, all male, called your attention to their merchandise. You could find everything there, vegetables, spices, gold, clothing, antiques, carpets and many more items, including relics of past ages. The whole area looked almost biblical and untouched by time. The souks opened every day, closed for prayers, and reopened right after. Shopping there was also a time to interact with the locals, which was intriguing, challenging and because of the language barrier, amusing for both the customer and the vendor. There was always a thrill in finding a great deal and bargaining for the best price so both parties were satisfied.

One of the many suggestions from the company was that we ladies should never venture out alone, especially to the souks. We respected their advice, however, we felt safe walking the narrow alleyways. With the vendors all male, women were outnumbered by the opposite sex. The men stared but we were accustomed to that and went about our business of haggling and buying. There was never a dull moment at the souks.

On one of our shopping days, I approached a clothing stall. The vendor's back was to me and when he turned around I was startled by a face literally covered with hair, but for two large protruding eyes. I immediately thought. "Good grief, the missing link!" In time, I became a regular customer because he gave me the best discounts. I once asked him how he went about pricing his merchandise, after noticing the way he always paused before telling me the cost, as if the price depended on how badly he thought I wanted the item and what I was willing to pay. The dear man had no idea how much to charge. He eventually trusted my discretion and explained. His broker in Europe would send a full container of miscellaneous items, with an invoice for the entire container, but no itemised price. He had no idea of the value of any individual piece of clothing, so he tried to assess your interest in the article, then suggest a price. Therefore, we ladies learned the trick when shopping was to act blasé; if not the price would be inflated, especially for us Westerners, and that was when some serious haggling occurred.

I bought Tazra's first communion outfit there, a lovely white embroidered Swiss dress, the gentleman had no idea of the quality. I paid fifty riyals (approximately twenty dollars) for what was actually worth one hundred dollars. I was grossly undercharged. However, the vendors were aware of our attraction to their antiques, Bedouin jewellery and artifacts and I'm sure the prices for those items were heavily inflated. Hence, haggling was more gruelling.

Everyone met and socialised at the souks. The women from different compounds, swapped information as to who gave the best discounts and where to find them. There was no map to the maze of shops, one had to find their own way by using landmarks, memory or vendor descriptions. For instance, my hairy-faced friend was dubbed "Merle's link guy". My best souking partner was my friend Carol Ann, her patience and humour throughout the heat and dust was admirable. Unfortunately, her sense of direction was worse than mine, which sometimes made shopping extra challenging.

Most companies supplied shopping buses for their employees' wives. Also, it was not unusual to see a Rolls Royce,

Bentley, or some other expensive vehicle pull up with Saudi ladies. Some men had no vehicles and rode bicycles or walked with their purchases strapped on their backs. This was when I learned that size does not determine strength. The strongest in my opinion were the small-framed men from Yemen, some not more than approximately 5 feet tall and weighing maybe 125 pounds, with items such as refrigerators, stoves, or large bags of rice on their backs. We watched in awe; the gentlemen displayed no discomfort and returned our looks with smiles.

I was especially fascinated with the spice souk. The blend of smells such as cloves, caraway seeds, cumin, camphor, myrrh, cinnamon, sandalwood and henna to name a few, including some twisted roots like turmeric, ginger and many unrecognisable herbs, were in abundance. They were piled high on wooden trays and some in open burlap bags. We bought few spices there, we had no idea what most of them were, only that they enhanced food, beauty or were for medicinal purposes; the variety was endless. A vendor once tried explaining the benefit of some dried leaves to my friend and I. We gathered from his limited English, and our very basic Arabic, that they were for feminine complications. However, his side of the conversation was becoming a little too graphic and so with a hasty "shukran" (thank you), we exited the area.

A couple of us ladies were once caught in a sandstorm while walking around the souks. As the wind swept through, the vendors were busy covering their spices. We started to look for an enclosed area and quickly realised there was none, for everywhere was open to the elements. By the time we diverted to our waiting bus, our hair, ears, nostrils and anywhere else that ground spices could have found shelter, became depositories for the airborne powders. We smelt like mobile spice vendors as we headed home to much needed showers.

Being caught in a sandstorm could be a frightening and painful experience. The skies become dark, like prior to a rainfall and one literally smells the dust before it actually appears. The wind approaches, bringing sand, debris and

Riyadh

dust. With limited visibility and the blowing sand stinging your face, one can easily become disoriented. Driving is dangerous and during a severe sandstorm aeroplanes are grounded, much like a snowstorm. Despite the heat, dust and haggling, we enjoyed shopping and socialising at the souks. Regretfully, most of the shops have since closed down because of the competition from the shopping malls which opened years later; that feeling of walking through narrow alleyways in 'past times' has disappeared. The old world charm lost.

Another unique experience was carpet buying. Aubrey's most enjoyable pastime was spent in the carpet stores. In Toronto we had to settle for two machine made Persian style rugs for our apartment. Therefore, one could well imagine how thrilled he was at seeing all the hand knotted carpet shops in Riyadh. And more so, he could now afford one! Throughout our years in the Kingdom, I always thought of Persian rugs as my one competition. Keeping Aubrey out of a carpet store was like trying to curb an endless affair.

Stepping inside a rug store was more like a visit to a friend's home. You were seated on sofas, offered tea, coffee, juice, water and dates, while discussing families or some sort of social event. The children amused themselves by climbing and jumping on the folded or rolled up carpets while we were presented with beautiful ones for our consideration.

With his usual light and casual gait, Aubrey was assiduous when walking around each carpet laid out at his feet. By noticing the wool, silk blend, colours and pattern, he could determine the area in Iran where they were made. He would then stoop down to check the knot density, weft, vegetable dye, and the family's name which was weaved into some. His knowledge about Persian rugs was impressive; this was acquired because of the hours spent socialising with the owners, brokers and handlers, over endless cups of tea.

Prior to negotiations, the salesman, who most times was the owner, was equipped with a calculator or pad would record the price. The pad was passed back and forth until an agreed price was met. Aubrey always ignored the original asking price and wrote down what he thought was a fair amount to start bargaining by saying, "We start from here". During the process, more small talk and pleasantries were exchanged, with more refreshments. If no agreement was met, you then had the option of taking the carpet home to help you decide. As mentioned, this was like visiting a friend and took three or four hours from beginning to end.

Within a few years, Aubrey developed the reputation as a rug *aficionado* and was always asked by friends and acquaintances for his advice before purchasing carpets. An American gentleman called one day asking for his 'services' regarding buying a high-quality carpet. Aubrey helped, at no cost, eager for any excuse to visit the carpet shops.

I was also amazed with the quality of such works of art. Some silk rugs had a knot density so high, they draped over your hand like brocade or fine tapestry. We left Saudi Arabia with enough carpets to furnish at least three or four houses, and when I sometimes fretted about the expenditure, Aubrey's assurance was always, "Regard it as our investment for retirement, love." Our girls and grandchildren grew up around carpets and appreciate them; Aubrey selected the ones he wanted to leave the grandchildren. As they grow older Aliya, Tazra or I will pass on the legacy of enlightening them – with our limited knowledge – about the quality and time involved in making such beautiful works of art. Aubrey was robbed of this pleasure, which I knew he was looking forward to doing himself.

Apart from beautiful rugs, another item Saudi Arabia sold in abundance was gold jewellery. The ladies favourite pastime was gold shopping. Before venturing out, we checked the world price of gold which was published daily in the newspaper. Then the phone would start ringing. "Gold is lower today! Let's go shopping!"

Stepping into the gold souk was an experience like no other, everything shining was gold. Jewellery hung from the walls, covered the counters, glass cabinets and was stacked on trays. My first encounter with traditional necklaces for Saudi brides was astounding. Artistic masterpieces and larger than any gold jewellery item I have ever seen. They adorned from neck to waist and were as wide as breastplates, but very delicately made, with intricate gold filigree floral designs. To display them properly, these necklaces were hung from the ceiling in the shops.

All of the jewellery was 18 to 21 carat and sold by weight and current world market price. No taxes or labour charges were attached to the item. Hence, buying gold jewellery in Saudi Arabia was a bargain. Back on the bus, after our shopping spree, we discussed prices and which vendor gave the best discounts, while purchases were passed back and forth the length of the bus, for scrutiny and admiration.

Like most countries in that part of the world, haggling is a way of shopping; it adds that bit of *je ne sais quoi* to purchasing. Aubrey tried to rationalise my negotiating skills. He claimed that I would haggle fiercely over five riyals, then tip the salesman ten. I explained that the five riyals I haggle over comes from the proprietor. I add my five for the salesman who works hard and was always pleased because of our appreciation for his service.

It so happened, my haggling habit followed me back to Canada. One day, I had an hour to spare prior to collecting the girls from school and went into a small boutique owned and operated by a French gentleman.

After admiring a lovely cream silk and chamois leather outfit, I tried it on. Both the blouse and skirt fitted beautifully but I hesitated, apart from not needing any more clothes, this one was expensive. I then thought, "With time to kill, why not haggle?" Surprisingly, the salesman brought the price down a little, which was enough encouragement for me to continue. After a few minutes – which must have felt like hours to him, with numbers going back and forth – the gentleman was so frustrated with my relentless counter offers, he eventually gave me a look of resignation, agreed to my price and said "Madame, do you want a job as my buyer? You are good!" I politely declined and promised to keep the offer in mind, should I need to seek employment.

Before handing over my credit card, I asked what percentage he pays the bank. I then suggested a cash deal if he reduced my purchase price again by half of the bank charges. I ended up convincing him that he was saving fifty percent on the transaction fees. He agreed and we completed the cash purchase.

Believe me, this gets better! The Gods must have been with me that day. As I was about to depart, I noticed very close to the door was a rack with colourful silk tank tops. I asked my friend – after an hour of haggling, also our shared love for his homeland, France, I considered us *amies* – for the price of the tops. He told me to take one. Shocked, I clarified his generosity. These were well made and good quality silk tops. He confirmed and insisted, "Mrs Miller, just take one and leave. It is my gift to you!"

A couple of ladies were just entering the store and I think he wanted me out of there. In anticipation of him rescinding his offer, along with my eagerness to get a free top, I did not linger over colours. It so happened, the one I selected looked more becoming on my sister-in-law, Pamela Mary, so I gave it to her.

While modelling my outfit for Aubrey that evening I related the incident. Much to my displeasure, he did not appreciate my haggling skills and I had to promise not to try that again. Unlike so many ladies, I am not that fond of shopping, but I thoroughly enjoy the challenge of haggling. Incidentally, I never succumbed to the temptation, I kept my promise. But, Oh, how my expat girlfriends and I missed the thrill of negotiating a good deal! The cajoling, the facial expressions and body language of haggling, is an art unto itself!

TWENTY-FOUR

After eight years in the Kingdom, we returned to Canada. Aliya had completed grade nine and the International School did not go beyond that. We didn't want to send her to boarding school and Aubrey still had a year to complete his contract, so he helped us relocate then returned to Saudi Arabia after a couple of months helping us settle in. Life in Canada took some getting used to, we managed but missed Aubrey terribly.

This is his first letter upon returning to Riyadh.

* * * * *

Riyadh, August 15/1987

Dearest,

It seems so strange returning to Riyadh without you guys in tow. The trip was not too bad, at least the parts that I remember. Between being tired and sad at leaving you guys behind, I was able to block out most of the journey. The terrible heat in Riyadh jolted me back to reality. Anyhow, here I am.
    Most of the folks are still on vacation, the compound is like a ghost town. As a result, there are not too many rumours I could pass on.
    So much for my rambling, I am well, though there are times when I question my sanity for being here. Work

keeps me distracted, the evenings and weekends are tough at times. Please don't worry, I am sure when I get into the routine of jogging etc. the loneliness will not be so bad.

How are you making out? Keep a close eye on the kids and let them know I love and miss them very much. Tell Aliya and Tazra the cats Mickey and Tiggy are well and have survived our departure. As for the rest of strays, I do not know how they are, I cannot muster the courage to check on them, since there is not much I could do.

This was supposed to be just a short note to let you know I am well, and here I've written more than I intended. Anyhow love, do take care of yourself and our girls. Remember, I love you very much. So long until I hear from you, love to the kids, the old lady, Mama and Papa.

Always yours,
Brey

His second letter.

* * * * *

Riyadh, August 21/1987

My Dearest,

I have passed my first week and it is really not too bad, except for the loneliness. For a person who has no commitments at home, it is a near perfect life. The houseboy keeps the place clean, laundry and dishes are washed, linens changed once a week, the food is not too bad, quite a variety of hot meals, milk, juice, drinks, etc. But when our family is split up, these things cannot compensate. Anyhow this is the best alternative to having Aliya go off to boarding school.

Everyone that you are acquainted with is alright, this of course, is based on an assumption, since I rarely see them. It is not entirely their fault; I have not made an effort to socialise as yet.

This is just a short letter to assure you I am well and surviving. Miss and love you guys very much. Take care of yourself and don't worry or work too much getting settled, all will be done in time. Kiss the kids for me and remind them of how much I love them, also tell them and yourself, that you three mean the most in the world to me, yes, even more than our carpets.

Love Ya!
Yours always, Brey

PS. Yes, I promise to stay away from the carpet shops.

This letter escaped the Time Capsule. I found it among Aubrey's belongings. The date confirms this was my first letter to him, after he returned to Riyadh to complete his contract. The irony is, I am now one of those "widowed people" I mentioned here.

* * * * *

November 14/1987

My darling Brey,

Life seems to be moving so slowly and getting nowhere for me. I miss you terribly and would never get accustomed to being away from you. Please don't worry, I'm doing all that I can regarding the house and trying not to sweat over the minor stuff. I can't seem to express myself as beautifully in my letters as you. I enjoy reading yours, your slight humour and much love. I sometimes

Hertfordshire, England, 1986

think how devastating our situation could have been, if this parting were permanent. How tough it must be for all the separated or widowed people in life. No material comfort is sufficient. It must be a terrifying feeling, when one's happiness is so dependent on another. Anyhow, I'm lucky to be blessed with you. I cannot promise to be more efficient, can't seem to curb the tendency to say something on every subject, still very impulsive, and not too slim or gorgeous looking. But I promise, my love will always be yours. No matter what life has in store for us, we will face it together.

On one of our trips to Paris, I don't recall when, strange how dates elude me but my heart remembers moments. I stood next to you on the Pont de la Concorde Bridge overlooking the Seine River. As some folks say, and I agree, "A bad day in Paris is better than a good day anywhere else." It was a cloudy and chilly afternoon, yet the feeling, romantic. How you occupied my heart! I reached for your hand, you understood and responded by gently squeezing my fingers. I then thought, "Could I love him more?" No, I gave you my all and still do. Your attention was focused on a bateau-mouche navigating down the river. And even without turning your head towards me, you sensed the expression on my face and said, "Don't look at me like that, Nastyface. This is not the time or place!"

Brey I want to hold you, talk with you. Yes, and other things too. I have never told you how I love watching you shave; I love seeing your hands on the steering wheel; I love hearing your delightfully sultry and sometimes teasing voice, during those special moments; I love you in white shirts, sleeves rolled up above your elbows; I love when we're saying goodbye to our visitors at the door, you wave with one hand, the other discreetly, well, you know where; I love watching you sitting at your desk, concentrating on whatever you're reading, the way your index and middle fingers move slowly back and forth across your forehead; I love the feel of your rough beard against my skin; I love how you refrain from displaying your affection when others are around, except a discreet wink or a slight brush of your hand across my bum; I love your knowledge, wisdom and patience while explaining whatever I need to understand; and I so love the way you hold me, firmly, and possessively.

Writing you makes me weepy, I've promised myself no more tears. After all, 42 years is too old for crying. One would think I was a young girl separated from her love for the first time.

I try not to think of the physical part of our relationship. Oh! But I do miss all the loving. You are quite the man, Miller! Take special care of yourself and in December I'll show you all that you've missed these past months. I'll be totally possessive; I have to get my fill of you. If it were possible, I would take you away for a few days but your visit will be too short.

Enough of my dreams and longings. I am fine, considering. I wouldn't say much for the girls, except that they are well, their letters I presume, tell all else. Mater and the rest of our relatives send their love and regards. So long dearest, please take care of yourself.

My love always and beyond,
Merle

* * * * *

Riyadh April 1/1988

My Dearest Merle,

As usual it was good talking with you and the girls this morning. Glad to hear the kids are trying their best academically. Keep encouraging them, you should let the school know of Aliya's decision to transfer to the five-year program. I wouldn't waste time writing about the weather, except that it is still bearable. I was over at Anastasia and Antoine for dinner on Wednesday, they sent their regards. I enjoyed the visit but my jogging was deferred, as you know my running is like my sex, they are both serious business with me, I do not respond kindly to those activities being disrupted.

By the time you receive this letter our 21st wedding anniversary will be history. One would think, that after 21 years of marriage and 100 years of aggravation, I would be glad to be away. But strangely enough, I cannot get used to this separated life. It is not the sex totally, I miss your company and our chats. Yes, I do miss the physical contact but I equally miss being with you, talking with you, doing things with you.

Coming back to our 21 years together. The total in my opinion is impressive. Basically, we have achieved most of what we hoped to and those which we haven't as yet,

I'm sure we will in the future. Of all our achievements, raising the girls without them having any hang ups and who seem to be developing into strong assertive young women, must be counted as our greatest. And I must say, even with all the frustrations, we have shared very good years.

Thank you my love, for twenty-one years of love, happiness, unselfishness, and damn good sex. I enjoy a lot of things in this world but the most enjoyable is —— — you! You have been a loving and caring wife, who has put my needs above yours, a good mother, who has given the kids the best you had to offer. For all of this I love and thank you. Hope the next twenty-one years are equally good.

Throughout my reflections, I couldn't help but smile when I remembered some of your better moments. Do you recall when you left my set of keys at your parents and we did not discover this until we lugged baby Aliya and the groceries upstairs. You borrowed my keys because you couldn't find yours, which was somewhere in our apartment. We then had to carry everything back to the car and drive to Ma and Pa. And the time you used the little money we allocated for a Christmas tree and bought me a sweater, which you hid under our bed and remained silent as I accused you of misplacing the money. Not forgetting the day you decided to go and bake our Christmas cake at Ma, you forgot the main ingredient, all the fruits, I then had to drive back in the snow and ice for it. Sometime back, I bought you that ruby and diamond ring, you took it to the jeweller to have it adjusted and didn't remember until almost a year later, then you couldn't find the paperwork to retrieve it. And I have lost count of the many flights you've missed. That's just to mention a few of those 'moments'. But above all, I remember the love you have given me, as well as the courage you showed to defy your parents and marry me. I was so proud of you when you decided to go to Montreal in March 1967 to tell them.

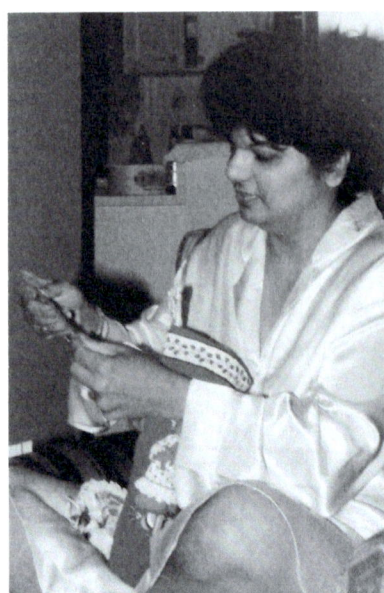

Christmas, Toronto, 1990, left, and Christmas, Toronto, 1989

Your love, courage and unselfishness are what I remember most and love you for. I have never met anyone as unselfish as you. It's a gift my love only few possess. I know I get on your case for your lackadaisical approach to some things but in the final analysis, it is your other qualities that invariably win the day. Always remember, in the midst of my ranting, I do love you, do not for one moment forget that.

It really is a joy when you have a partner whom you thoroughly delight in pleasing, right now if you were here I would ———————. See what you bring out in me? I shouldn't be writing this stuff on Good Friday, so before I continue to sin, I'll close with lots of love to you and request that you tell our girls, I love and miss them. Looking forward to taking you in my arms in May.

Always yours,
Brey

Aubrey later replaced the ruby and diamond ring, it will now be passed on to our granddaughter Ruby. And I remember a couple of my "missed flights", the others, I have conveniently blocked out.

I was scheduled to fly from London to Toronto, when my nephew arrived at my brothers' home to drive me to Heathrow Airport. I wasn't even dressed. Realising I'd never make the flight, I called the airline and told them of the emergency I had. In a very sympathetic voice, the representative expressed how sorry she was to hear of my sister's illness. She immediately rescheduled me to fly out the following day, providing of course, my sister was better and I felt comfortable leaving her. The British, always so polite and most times, kind!

I never told Khalda that story. Arriving at her home in Toronto a couple of days later, I hugged her, looked up to the heavens, asked for forgiveness, and my sister's continued good health. As usual, when Aubrey heard I missed another flight, I got a telling off.

TWENTY-FIVE

A year later, Aubrey completed his contract and returned to Bell Canada in Toronto and once again our family was together in one place. After a couple of years Aliya went on to university and Tazra had one more year of high school. Aubrey left Bell for a job with Cantel, which later became Rogers.

Sometime in 1991, he received a phone call from three Saudi Telecom employees who were in Toronto, and he met them for dinner one evening. They asked what would it take to get him back to work with Saudi Telecom. Not taking them seriously, Aubrey laughingly listed off what that would entail. To his surprise, they immediately accepted. He was flabbergasted and refused to shake hands on the deal until he could discuss it with me and the girls. He came home at 2am and asked if I would like to return to the Kingdom. In my half-awake state, I asked, "Why and when?" We had never considered returning and were settled in Toronto. His reply was, "Go to sleep love, we'll talk later."

We discussed it later that morning, Aliya was home for the weekend, so we all sat down and talked. Our main concern was the girls and they were both in agreement that we should go. Aubrey would leave in January or February of 1992, while I remain with Tazra until she left for university. Within that year we would see each other at least three times. Aubrey also explained, the company would grant the girls resident status and bring them in twice a year. Of course, we would benefit from the usual perks that went with being an expat, also, a few of our friends were still there. I guess we convinced each other into going.

The girls and I knew Aubrey enjoyed working in the Kingdom but would never return unless he was convinced that we were all on board with the plan. After many discussions he accepted his new job. The girls and I visited twice within the year and Aubrey also made a trip home.

* * * * *

February 1992

My dearest Merle,

Do not worry about me, I am doing great under the current circumstances. Arthur, Peter and I hang out, sometimes Ben and Sayman join us. As a matter of fact, last Friday I bought Indian food and had them over, Mona and Terry were also here, Mona is eagerly awaiting your arrival. Last night I went to a dinner sponsored by the Canadian Businessmen Association, it was held at the Marriott hotel. The guest speaker was a war correspondent, by the name of North, his first name escapes me at the moment. He's Canadian and a friend of Peter Jennings, NBC anchorman. North started his career in Vietnam and is currently a news consultant to Prince Khalid the Saudi General who commanded the Allied forces during the Gulf conflict. North spoke well and is a very friendly bloke. All in all, a pleasant evening.

Looking forward to your coming. Be sure to confirm your flight three days prior to travelling. I know you're not too fond of coming via JFK but as your ticket is being paid for by the company, we have no choice. You will have to use Delta business class lounge, as Saudia's is not completed as yet. If your flight is anything like mine, it should be pleasant. Be sure to have lots of reading material.

If you have the space, could you please bring a couple of my suits, the grey Paco Rabanne and the Christian Dior grey with blue stripes also my dark blue jacket, the one I had made in England and a few ties, I leave the choice of ties to you. Now, only if you have the space, no problem if you can't bring them.

It is still cold and as a result, I haven't started to jog as yet. Incidentally, have you given the money to Herbie? And did you remember to order the catalogue? I know, I have made a pest of myself. I had better sign off before you blow your stack. Before I close, allow me to tell you how much I love and miss you. Oh! Oh! You won't? OK, then I won't!!!!!!

Keep yourself warm for me! Luv Ya!

As always, your loving husband and Man,
Brey

Aubrey, always the impeccable dresser, loved fine clothes. A quote he used, maybe to justify his extravagance on buying anything, was "I'm too poor to buy cheap." He passed away leaving an entire wardrobe, from casual to formal wear which I had to sort through when I was moving. I ended up giving most away, the girls kept some of the classic wear. The movers got ostrich and fine Italian leather shoes. My friend Val took about two dozen suits to distribute to those in need. I had five of his shirts made into teddy bears by volunteers at The Doane House Hospice and I donated some money on behalf of our grandchildren in memory of their Grandy. His rings, cufflinks, watches, pens and other personal items are for our grandchildren at his request, on momentous occasions like birthdays and graduations. Everything else was given away.

I found a few of my letters to him. This one I wrote while I remained in Canada prior to Tazra going off to University.

* * * * *

March 4/1992

My darling Brey,

We are apart again, however it's only a physical separation. You invade my thoughts constantly. This restless love, the longing to see you, hold you, feel your arms around me. I just remembered a comment you made the last time we went to the mall. I called your attention to a couple holding hands and jokingly asked, "How come we don't hold hands much when walking?" You replied, "Only if you are in danger of falling on your face." So romantic!!

    Anyhow Miller, I hope you settle in nicely and are enjoying the sunshine. I'm already counting the days, I can't wait to join you. I pray God continues to protect you. If not for your sake, then mine, for my other half is lost without you. I love the person you are, despite your ability to aggravate my soul with your impatience and your need for perfection, you are still, my everything! Throughout our debates, arguments and regardless of how difficult a situation I am confronted with, four attributes sustain me. The knowledge that we love each other unconditionally; you are dependable; I trust you totally; and without any verbal assurances, I always feel safe and secure in your keeping. You know how to ease my troubled mind, soar my heart that it reaches such heights. I swear sometimes I don't deserve you but God must like me some, to bless me with you and our girls. I envy no one, I have all!

    Thanks again, for the beautiful long-stemmed roses, all forty-seven of them. Now that I've borne my heart and soul, I'll close with my love and devotion.

My love always and beyond,
Merle

TWENTY-SIX

Tazra went on to university and I joined Aubrey in Riyadh. Life was beautiful. The girls were happy and well, we spoke with them regularly. We ended up living seventeen more years in the Kingdom, returning to Toronto twice a year and the girls also joined us every year until they were married.

Within those years Aubrey left Saudi Telecom and worked as a consultant with Detecon, of Deutsche Telekom Group (German) and later, Norconsult Telematics (Norwegian) firms. The girls were settled in University and Aubrey and I seemed to rediscover each other. Those early years of marriage adjusting to a new country, school, parenthood and coping with limited funds were hectic. Now life afforded us time to search our souls, appreciate our surroundings, and on the whole, enjoy a leisurely lifestyle.

We didn't need an event, place or excuse to be together. Anytime, anywhere, was peaceful, happy and loving. Aubrey and I shared a great friendship, the saying "One must like the person one loves" applied to us. I always thought of our lives as a blending of souls and was amazed by how much we had in common. At the same time, how much we niggled each other. I also wondered if, in some ways I became like him, or he me, and felt that a union as ours comes only once in a lifetime. The average lifespan, in my opinion, too short to recapture such love and camaraderie.

We shared many amusing moments. For instance, one Friday after lunch while relaxing, reading and listening to some music, an old catchy instrumental 60s tune came on.

Knowing Aubrey didn't have an ear for most music, except a bit of light classical and jazz, I challenged him: "If you name that tune, I'll give you anything you want." My husband lifted his head and asked seriously, "Anything?" Feeling the confidence of a person holding a Royal Flush, I confirmed boldly, "Anything within my power!" He paused for a moment, listening to the tune, then continued reading his book, dismissing both me and the music.

A couple of hours later, he approached me in the kitchen and said, "Wheels". My jaw dropped with surprise. Aubrey then said, "OK! Time to deliver; let's go upstairs!" While climbing the stairs reluctantly, I fretted, "I'm not in the mood for this." Aubrey replied, "Never mind, I'll get you in the mood." He later claimed, "I'm available and willing to accept any more challenges!" I never underestimated my husband's repertoire in music again.

On one of my visits to Canada, even with the anticipation of seeing the girls, I felt sad that Aubrey couldn't accompany me. I also wanted to remind him again, how much I truly love and respect him.

Even after so many years together, I still left notes, letters or quotations, which were placed in his drawers, jacket pockets, wallet etc. The following was left on his pillow, to be found after dropping me off at the Riyadh airport. I also included a CD of Jennifer Rush's "The Power of Love".

* * * * *

Riyadh, September 1998

Darling Brey,

My renaissance man, so complete and everything I love. Being away from you is always an inconvenience to my heart. You may never know how very blessed I feel to be entangled in your life. You have a kind soul, I appreciate the way you take care of me, ensuring I am well, and how tenderly and patiently, when I am not. I have even grown to accept your impatience and your need for perfection. Sometimes secretly smiling when I think your reaction to some moments, exaggerated. I couldn't bear tolerance or indifference in our relationship, that would bore me and my love, 'boredom' is never a word to describe us. I need an Aubrey to curb my spontaneity and excessive chatting. I know you indulge me most times but I also know where you draw the line.

You are very much your own man. And I do love that in you! I love your pride and sometimes – note the operative word here, 'sometimes' – your arrogance. I also respect your need for privacy and your passion for justice. I could elaborate on your 'quick-tempered' behaviour. But then, I bring out most of it in you. So, we will not venture down that lane. On many occasions, I observed you with pride and admiration, as you stood alone with your convictions, even when the odds were against you.

Above all, I love your total commitment as a father to our girls and remember every moment you've spent with them. Most fathers are good. You however, are the epitome of fatherhood, with your extra touch of love and wisdom.

As we approach our twilight years, I pray they are long and healthy ones. Rediscovering life's beauty one day, through the eyes of our grandchildren and reflecting on our years together. Always with joy, peace and love in our hearts. This will be sufficient for me and I hope for you. Our life together is good. Thank God!

Friday is a day of rest in the Kingdom. Weekends are Thursdays and Fridays, the first business and school day of the week is Saturday. We started to do our weekly grocery shopping on Friday mornings, we found it quiet and the bread freshly baked. During one of our shopping days, Aubrey was in another aisle of the supermarket, I was waiting for the bread to complete baking while chatting with the baker. He showed me some photographs of his recent marriage in Bangladesh. To my surprise, he also handed me a letter from his parents, thanking us for the money we gave him. It allowed them to buy sixty-five chickens for the wedding meal and they mentioned how proud they felt for not having to serve their guests a vegetarian dinner. I was not aware of giving him any money but did not indicate so, simply because I knew of my husband's kindness and generosity.

While driving home I asked Aubrey about it and he said that a couple of months ago they were discussing the young man's forthcoming wedding plans. Knowing most Bangladeshis were Muslims and not vegetarians, he asked why meat wasn't being served. The baker said his parents couldn't afford it, so Aubrey contributed a few hundred riyals towards the traditional wedding dinner of "chicken biryani". I wondered if Aubrey thought I would have objected to him giving the money, for he didn't mention it. He said, "I knew you wouldn't have minded. I just thought it was between the guy and myself." That was typical of my thoughtful husband, he went about helping quietly without stripping anyone of their pride or dignity. One of Aubrey's best qualities was his giving heart, which was unknown to most.

About weddings! I love attending marriage celebrations. What is there not to enjoy? Most ceremonies move me to tears, especially the long romantic and eloquent vows couples now promise to each other.

Aubrey and I had committed to the thousand year old 'To love, honour and obey.' I don't know much about the traditions and culture regarding Bangladeshi weddings. However, Saudi weddings are most enjoyable and interesting. During our years in the Kingdom we attended a few, and because of the climate, most celebrations, or rather all, start at 11pm and conclude at 3-4am. Male and female guests celebrate separately. Aubrey and I always decided on an approximate time to leave.

When we arrived at our destination, he used a separate entrance and we didn't see each other until we departed. The ladies dressed elegantly, their little daughters just as beautifully outfitted and the sons celebrated with their fathers. Ladies have their own all female band and indulge in lots of dancing, accentuating on their hips by using scarfs, which was always supplied by the hostess and placed close to the band. When the guests were in the mood for dancing, they selected a scarf, tied it around their hips, then proceed to gyrate to the rhythm. According to Aubrey, the male guests partook in the sword dance.

We ladies had the honour of greeting the groom when he brought his bride gifts of gold jewellery contained in a chest and guarded by an old and trusted great-aunt. The male guests never saw or met the bride.

The first Bedouin wedding I attended was enlightening, especially when the meal was served; it was a flavourful rice and lamb dish, *kapsa*. It was served on huge round platters which were placed on the carpet-covered ground with approximately eight guests to each platter. A little uncarved roasted lamb, complete with head and eyes intact, laid across the rice. My first reaction was sympathy for the lamb, this was quickly dispelled as the ladies started to eat. The lamb was cooked to perfection, moist and tender, so was the flavoured rice, which was garnished with tiny cubes of halloumi cheese and raisins. Plates, cutlery or furniture of any type were not an option, and we ate only with our right hands, as is customary. The meal was delicious. However, I ate very little, one had to get accustomed to dining Bedouin style.

Also, a habit that took me many years to acquire was also eating such a heavy meal at one or two o'clock in the morning. Abstaining would have been considered an insult.

A couple of other weddings we attended were held at five-star hotels and the meals were both western and eastern. I enjoyed all the weddings, but the Bedouin celebrations were my most memorable. Guests are not expected to give a wedding present. However, when you visit the newlyweds in their home, it is customary to take a housewarming gift.

Saudi homes are set up with two living and dining rooms, so the same segregation was applied when we visited our friends. I rarely met our host and Aubrey never met the hostess. The houses on our compound were western style, so when we reciprocated, Aubrey took the men to a restaurant while I entertained the ladies at home. After the visit, I escorted the wives back to their car and chauffeur; Aubrey was never in their presence. This bit of inconvenience never bothered us, for we believed, "When in Rome"!

TWENTY-SEVEN

After losing Aubrey, I felt closest to him in the small hours of early morning. Waking just before dawn, and missing him more than any other time of the day, I reach for my iPad, which is always on my nightstand, and write and write!

* * * * *

November 7/2016

My Love,

I miss you terribly today. Through some divine or mysterious way, I think you are aware of my feelings. My heart is weary with emotions so vibrant. Sometimes I long for memories to fade a little, they can be painful, both good and bad. How does one control one's thoughts? I want to stop feeling and start thinking. Brey, I'm so mixed up! The hurt and longing seems endless, especially during the fall months, as you know, my favourite season. Now looking at the profusion of colourful leaves, and feeling the early morning mist on my face just brings deep sadness. Life does not share well but I have to be grateful for the years spent with you. And one day, I'll appreciate again, every leaf on every tree, with all the wonder and beauty of autumn.
    The girls are as well as can be, we speak every day, mostly in the mornings, that's the toughest time of day

for me. At the break of dawn, like today, I look out the window and up to the sky as if willing you to appear, smile and tell me all is well with both of us. I keep my morning moments close to my heart, they are beautiful, comforting and sometimes sad. That's the time I feel closest to you and also have my chats with God. I wouldn't refer to those moments as praying. Repetition of all the prayers we grew up with seems like I don't want to think for myself. But Brey, I do want to think, reason, question, and plead. Then when I settle into bed in the evenings, I ask for forgiveness, just in case I went about it all wrong. I always thank Him for the years you were on loan to me. Also, to continue overlooking and blessing you.

Living without you is existing, with major and minor adjustments. That's OK, the adjusting keeps me occupied and I have to use my brain. 'Brain', that's the organ you teased me about being born without. Strangely, simple little things, like zipping up my dress, I find difficult; I have worn a dress with a zipper at the back only once since you've passed away. I know I have to master that frustration one day.

While on the subject about zippers, I remember the many times we arrived late when visiting anyone. I was always blamed by our hostess. Everyone thought of you as the organised and punctual one. Little did they know! Instead of zipping up my dress, you just couldn't understand how it sometimes ended on the floor, "Slipped through my fingers" you always claimed. On one occasion I remembered protesting, "Brey, no! We'll be late." You replied, "Yes, now shut up and enjoy!" I did, by then oblivious to the fact that I'll be blamed, again! I still smile when I recall an event Joy and Manny invited us to, we arrived late. Joy greeted us, handed me a drink and said accusingly, "You are late!" I told her it was your fault. She looked at you questionably. You returned her look with raised eyebrows and a straight face. Remember what you said? "I have no idea what Merle is implying.

As usual, I was on top of the situation, ready and waiting for her!" I nearly choked on my drink. That statement went right over Joy's head. I was forever amazed as to how you manipulated the English language!

Then about finances, my mathematical reasoning tells me I have sufficient funds. Having never worried about money before, even during your student days, I now find it a bothersome task. You always fretted about me not getting involved with our finances. Now I don't have a choice or excuse, I have to deal with it. I don't suppose you could continue managing the money from where you are? I must remember to discuss that possibility with God when next we talk. We share some tough thoughts, God and I, believe me, there are times when our relationship seems muddled and disheartening, those are the moments when my faith wavers. Regardless of my frame of mind I constantly ask him to take care of you. I seem to be asking God for so much of late! However, after realising I've taken too much liberty with my wants and expectations, I immediately beg for forgiveness. Contrary to my moments of doubt, I believe in him and hope he hears me. After all, I am a good person. I know you beg to differ. I am aware of my shortcomings and make no excuses for them. After all Miller, think how bored you would have been if I were an, "O.K, dear", wife. But because you knew my heart, you overlooked my faults – sometimes! It was always wonderful and comforting to know that in spite of my imperfections, I was enough for you!

There is so much more I want to tell you. I recall the many topics we discussed, laughed and argued about. I miss our daily chats, especially while sitting alone with my pot of tea. I remember and sometimes smile or weep. I have to believe we'll be together again. It keeps me sane.

Everyone is kind and thoughtful. I am surviving my love, so don't worry. Ken is most supportive, he sends me parables, quotations, music etc. Always some message of hope and encouragement. We speak often and when I want to talk, yes, like most times, he listens to my ramblings or sobs with great indulgence, even when I know he's had enough. Also, your long-time friend Lauren, she called one evening when my thoughts were in an incredibly sad place. Lauren talked, listened and prayed until I regained my composure. Not forgetting Vonnie, who is always at the other end of the line, regardless of the time. As you know she and I go way back to the days when I snuck away to meet you, my true alibi she was, and of course, my siblings and I speak often. As expected, Aliya and Tazra are always around, we find some comfort in each other. Thank God for all the good people in my life. I am indeed a fortunate lady.

Will write again soon. Bless you my darling and wherever you are my love and thoughts are with you.

My love always and beyond,
Merle

* * * * *

November 5/2017

My dearest Brey

I moved into my condominium suite and am still settling in. As you are aware, I've never lived on my own. Just as well I had so much to do, no time to indulge in that lost empty feeling. It was indeed a big job distributing some of our items. I kept what I could accommodate, the girls took what they wanted and I gave a few large pieces of furniture away. Brey, I held on to so many items which I will never use again but I can't seem to part with them. They are memories of you, me and our life together. Most folks kept advising me to get rid of what cannot be accommodated in the condo. They never understood most

Toronto, 2004

items came with a story and parting with any piece was reliving that story, which at most times, is painful. The realty guy asked if I would consider selling some of our art. He particularly liked the miniature painting you bought me in India. Of course, I said no, especially to that piece. Do you recall when we stayed at the Imperial Hotel in New Delhi? The shop downstairs had some fantastic works of art. We looked, admired and left, not interested in buying anything. That evening as we were getting dressed to go to dinner, I came out of the bathroom and there on the bed was this lovely painting. As I protested about you buying it, you said I looked at that particular one a little longer. So, while I was in the shower, you went down and bought it. As you were going into the bathroom, I remember saying, "Love, you are always buying me such beautiful things, I appreciate them but it's not necessary." Without stopping or turning around, you shrugged your shoulders nonchalantly and replied. "You know if possible, I'll buy you heaven." When I recall that incident, I regret not letting you know that your answer touched the very core of my soul. It was so profound, I was lost for words. Just as well you disappeared into the bathroom, for I stood dumbfounded, holding my painting. My darling Brey, you understood, that even wanting for ourselves, we wanted much more for the other. The laws of love I guess!

Our trip to India was spectacular, my 60th birthday gift from you. You said it was also the honeymoon we never had. Sixteen days in the north. You arranged the entire luxurious trip in detail. It was educational, adventurous and so romantic. I especially enjoyed our moonlight supper in the middle of the lake, on the barge. The only light was from the moon, stars and a few candles. The scent of fresh flowers everywhere, even the floor was covered with petals. Soft music, and our dinner being delivered by launch, course after course, the waiters served each course then departed with the launch. I remember looking at you across the table, admiring your tastefully casual attire. And being caught up in the romantic atmosphere, do you recall I said, "You're so darn handsome, how I love you and you're mine, all mine!" You replied with a wicked grin, as the back of your hand caressed my cheek, "Yours, just for now my love, I have a date with our maître d' later this evening. The same one whom you claim ignores you as she tells me about her India, while her flirting eyes say otherwise." Just God, you and me. You never failed to surprise me! You knew that although I didn't get you many material things, my love enfolded you, it was enduring, reliable, devoted, and whatever I needed to do to keep you happy, I did with pleasure. Do you remember, after all the romantic gestures and declarations, we ended up talking about Leo, our first – at that time – grandchild.

    I will stop writing now, maybe I'll be able to sleep for a couple of hours. Oh, it sounds like rain! What wouldn't I give to spend another rainy day with you!

I will always love you Aubrey Miller.
Merle

India was magical and worth the headache and aggravation of getting from Toronto to New Delhi. We spent Christmas of 2005 in Toronto with the girls and their families and then departed for Riyadh on the 28th of December.

    Upon arrival in Riyadh at about 1.00 am on the 30th, we were told our luggage was left in Frankfurt and would be on the next flight the following evening. After being airborne for fourteen hours, with seven hours time difference and the relief of being on *terra firma* again, we did not need to hear such news. Everything for our trip was packed in those suitcases, including items purchased in Toronto in anticipation of the vacation. Even worse, later that morning we were scheduled to fly out to New Delhi. One could imagine the conundrum! We arrived at our villa early in the morning, got out more suitcases and packed second choice clothing. On our way to the airport to catch our 9am flight, we asked our friend to have our delayed luggage delivered at his place that evening.

    After a short flight, we were greeted at the Indira Gandhi International Airport in New Delhi by our guide and a chauffeured large four wheel drive vehicle, stocked with refreshments. We spent the first two nights at the Imperial Hotel in New Delhi, in pure luxury, which was most welcomed after the previous forty eight hours. The corridors were decorated with impressive paintings, fine antique furniture and fresh orchids throughout. The receptionist escorted us to our room where she registered us as we sipped cool refreshing drinks. Our room was lovely, the bed was beautifully made up with embroidered Porthault linens and very comfortable. There was a large, deep bathtub, along with everything else to make one feel pampered. We relaxed and enjoyed two days of comfort and culinary delights with the anticipation of another couple of days at The Imperial before leaving New Delhi.

After our brief sojourn, we headed to the Indian states of Uttar Pradesh and Rajasthan.

In Agra we visited the Red Fort, sometimes referred to as "Agra Fort." Its beauty and history was overshadowed by the majestic Taj Mahal. Seeing the Taj Mahal took my breath away and I knew Aubrey felt the same. He silently walked around with all the wonder in his eyes. I was vocal, as usual. It was much larger than anticipated and we marvelled at the workmanship of this elaborately carved white marble structure. Inside was just as beautiful with the mausoleums of Mumtaz Mahal and her husband Shah Jahan. We also had a clear view of the monument from our hotel suite. The last sight before retiring for the night and the first at the break of dawn, was the glorious Taj Mahal, as it gleamed at dusk and dawn when it reflected the light. This tribute to true love was the main highlight of our trip.

Jaipur, known as the 'Pink City' because all the buildings are painted pink in honour of Prince Albert's visit in 1876, was another interesting city. We visited the Amer Fort, which was situated on a high hill and more accessible by elephant. While our guide was making the arrangements for the ride, we looked closely at the animals. Both Aubrey and I were appalled at their apparent sadness and resignation as tourists climbed on and off, while snapping photos. Such beautiful, sensitive mammals – my favourite animal – walking on gravel and what looked like concrete, in the blazing sun. Aubrey tore up our tickets, much to the horror of our guide. Refusing that mode of transport, we decided to walk and bore the heat and discomfort.

India, 2006

The long trek was worth it. Made of marble and sandstone, the palace overlooked the entire city. The impressive courtyards, each with its own entrance and history, needed more than one visit to appreciate the beauty of the architecture. Regretfully, time did not permit us the extended pleasure of returning before our departure. We also spent a night in the city of Bikaner. So much to see but so little time! Aubrey had planned a safari night for us in Jaisalmer that was most entertaining. It was a cultural evening with local entertainment including camel rides, dancing girls and a delicious dinner of regional cuisine.

India, 2006

India is also a shoppers' paradise. Beautiful jewellery, silk and cotton clothing, shawls, leather, cashmere and embroidered materials; the selection is truly beyond one's imagination. One day, after a couple of hours shopping, we both had enough. Feeling hot and tired, all I wanted was to sit in a cool place with a cup of tea. Our guide took us to a little hut, just as it started to rain. A friendly little old lady served us our tea. After I drank mine, she turned my demitasse cup upside down and offered to read my fortune. According to the fortune teller, "the leaves never lie." Aubrey did not partake in what he referred to as, "hocus-pocus". I was told by my reader of living a long and healthy life and of crossing many waters in the world. With all the travelling we were doing, I then thought, some things have already come to pass. She also predicted a few more pleasantries to look forward to. I paid for the reading and we departed.

Just as I stepped out of the door, my right foot landed in a puddle of water, deep and muddy enough to ruin my sandals. It had rained heavily while we were having our tea. Aubrey was in his element and said, "Instead of crossing the water, you landed into it, ruined your sandals and ended up paying for your mishaps!" He laughed and teased me relentlessly, while I fumed.

After sightseeing all day, visiting palaces, forts, havelis and shopping, we looked forward to coming back to the luxury of our hotel for a shower and high tea in the beautiful gardens among the flowers and peacocks. Later in the evening, we dined in one of the many restaurants while enjoying the entertainment.

For sixteen days and fifteen nights Aubrey and I soaked up the history, cuisine and thoroughly enjoyed the warm and friendly people from the State of Rajasthan, Agra and New Delhi. And how he and I laughed and loved! My birthday gift and the thirty five years of waiting for our honeymoon were worth every second. To have imagined or wanted more was inconceivable!

TWENTY-EIGHT

October 7/2018

Hi My Love,

I was just speaking with Marie yesterday. She is always curious about our life in Saudi Arabia. This time she asked about our Christmases there. As you are aware, in the seventies and eighties, we did crazy things to entertain ourselves. As I thought of our holidays in the Kingdom, everything started to unfold. The happy, funny and nostalgic times we shared with our friends. Of course, we women had lots of time for everything. Even with a comfortable life on the compound, missing our relatives and friends was a major setback.

Remember our 'once a month girls' night?' You guys babysat, while we ladies took turns getting together in each other's home. One September, having just returned from our holidays in Canada and elsewhere, we were feeling a bit low and missed our relatives and friends back home. Our discussion led to who was going where for the Christmas holidays. It seemed that everyone was going to a different country. The way we were feeling and the fact that most of us were going to spend the holidays in a foreign hotel, prompted us to celebrate Christmas then and there. With only one-week R&R, and the time difference, Canada was too far, most folks went to Europe or the Far East. You and I were fortunate, that year we celebrated ours in England, with Arif and the family at their home, Ayot Lodge; we had a fantastic time. Anyhow, Sharon – our hostess – brought out her tree, decorations, lights, Christmas music, candles and the works. We decorated her home fit for the season, while listening and singing along to the holiday music. I must mention the Riyadh red or white enjoyed by most of the girls helped keep the festive spirits up; I always abstained. Remember how horrified Jana always was when I diluted their wine with 7UP? As you know, the only vin I enjoyed in Riyadh was Charlie's. Our dear Swiss friend Charlie, who has now passed away. He always made me a few bottles of sweet red, labelling it, 'For Merle'. Some of the ladies who brought in goodies for the holidays went home and got them, we ate, drank, danced and had a great holiday night, returning to our villas in the early hours of that September morning, tired but happy.

You men had your crazy times too. Like the year when a few of the guys went down Chicken Street – aptly named by the expats, for the entire street sold chickens, live and dead – bought a live one, hung the recipe for chicken soup and a stock cube around the bird's neck and tied it in Chuck's backyard. Christmas morning, Marijke, his little girl, who asked Santa for a budgie, thought the jolly man made a mistake. That chicken became a well-fed bird by all the kids around, then suddenly disappeared. Rumour had it that a Bedouin had jumped the wall and absconded with the bird. I don't believe that. With the aroma of chicken soup in the air, I think that recipe was used after all.

As you may recall, years later for those who stayed in the Kingdom for the Christmas holidays, festive goodies and limited decor were available as large supermarkets opened and stocked up. Celebrations were contained on compounds or at the embassies. Do you recall the year we had a Christmas dinner in the desert, away from civilisation? That was the best, don't you agree? We were not told of the destination until a few hours prior to leaving, when maps were handed out with directions such as "pass the old discarded Mercedes on the right, then left after the huge boulder." With such explicit directions we had no problems locating our Christmas venue. One of the many five-star hotels catered the turkey dinner with all the trimmings. This was trucked in along with the white linens, candles, flowers, and Christmas decor, all set up under a huge white marquee. It was also the closest we got geographically of recreating that special time in Bethlehem. After our meal and much carolling, amidst the excitement of the children's laughter and cheer, we heard bells ringing in the distance. As the sound grew louder, we saw Santa riding a camel with red bags filled with toys. It was magical, not only for the kids but also us adults.

We must not forget the Christmas bazaars at the embassies or compounds, with ornaments, food and music from around the world, mingling with our international friends, exchanging food and presents. And in the early eighties you and I hosted our open house Christmas Eve. Our friends, including Lydia and Peter and their kids, celebrated many a Xmas Eve with us. We joined them sometimes for New Year's Eve dinner, and the traditional and delicious Dutch Oliebollen and I remember the year Dina, Mr Q, the kids and uncle were our house guests. We shared so many international dishes with our friends. How you enjoyed the savoury turnovers I made every year. While baking them you tasted a few as they came out of the oven; by the time I'd completed, half was eaten. Without saying anything to you, I always doubled up the recipe. Come dinner time you would claim, "I'll skip dinner tonight, somehow I'm not hungry." I usually just smiled. It was a pleasure seeing how you enjoyed them. Unlike me, you were not much of a foodie, so I tried to prepare whatever you enjoyed. Those pastries were always made with you in mind. I have not made them since you have passed away, maybe one Christmas in the future.

Then in the nineties when Aliya and Tazra came into the Kingdom for the holidays. Christmas Eve was always at Jana and Richard's home. A very European eve. Baby Jesus brought us all gifts and we sat down to good company, enjoyed Richard's great selection of music and a scrumptious seafood dinner, followed by the traditional cookies. Always, warm hospitality, wrapped up with love and that special touch of Czech flavour. Christmases with our international friends were most enjoyable and interesting. We discussed our different holiday traditions, foods, etc. and would have been perfect, had our relatives and friends from Canada been there. As you are aware, our Christmas tree here in Canada is a conversation piece when we have guests over. Ornaments from over twenty-five countries. Our grandchildren select a couple each Christmas for themselves.

Marie and I also chatted about you, she mentioned how she always admired you. Now, don't let that go to your head! Remember Marie is my 'religious' friend and it was meant platonically, I think!!

Will close now my love. Incidentally, have you had enough of reading what you already know? I never get tired of relating all. So, put up darling! What else do you have to do up there anyway?

My love always and beyond,
Merle

One Christmas, Aubrey and I decided not to exchange presents. He claimed, "You already have all the rocks. Diamonds, sapphires, rubies and emeralds." I agreed and we bought each other books and a few trinkets. Christmas night, as I entered our dimly lit bedroom, a string was tied from his bedside lamp, across the bed to mine, with a little gift-wrapped box hanging over my pillow. I protested, "Brey, we decided no presents!" His reply, "It's just a small rock." I immediately turned on the light. Aubrey knew how I loved opening presents from him; he never failed to surprise me and this time was no different. It was indeed a rock, which he picked up from outside. His first words, after seeing the way I took it out of the box, were, "I washed it." A few minutes later, while we were occupied with other matters, I felt him slip a ring on my finger. I sprung up and turned on the light. It was a green garnet and white sapphire ring. While admiring my present, Aubrey promptly pulled me back in his arms, swore quietly and said, "I should have given you the ring later ... much later!" On one of his trips to Zurich, he brought me back a box of champagne truffles. Watching the delight on my face, he commented, "Amazing how you show the same enthusiasm receiving a few chocolates, as you do a piece of jewellery."

During his student years, I saved quarters in a jar and I must have mentioned, as a child I always wanted a savings bank in the shape of a pig. My guy obviously retained that useless bit of information because much to my surprise, while coming home via Heathrow Airport – and I'm sure on a whim – he bought me a Lynx silver piggy bank which he filled with my favourite chocolates. Now, looking at my little pig on the tallboy, I smile as my fingers slide along the cold metal. Aubrey seemed to have remembered every discussion between us, trivial or relevant. Whatever he got me over the years was chosen with much thought. He especially liked giving me jewellery and knew my taste well; they are all beautiful, but not always a priority for me. On many occasions, I was tempted to say something naughty like, "I love diamonds my darling, but take me to that place where our bodies merge, in pure bliss." I never did though. His presents were wrapped with so much love, humour would not have been appropriate at that moment. With his passing, went my interest in jewellery. I hardly wear any now.

TWENTY-NINE

We moved back to Canada in 2009, just in time for Ruby, our last grandchild's birth. Aubrey arrived a month later. Relocating was comfortable and easy. The grands were a total joy, we were involved in the usual concerts, grandparent's tea, Halloween, birthdays and everything that involved grandchildren. We had purchased a plot of land in Barbados, intending to build a house for the winter months. Then the grands came along and upset that applecart. Being with them was such a pleasure, Barbados seemed a lifetime away. We abandoned the paradise island for time spent with our four munchkins.

Aubrey's new career – 'Improvement Projects' as he referred to them – kept him happy and busy around the house. An electrical engineer whose heart belonged in our garage, where he carved, sawed and painted things to enhance our home. He also ripped up our ensuite bathroom floor, laid down heating elements and retiled with marble. He redesigned our library, Georgian style, with custom built floor to ceiling bookshelves, and completed countless other renovations. Being a perfectionist with limited knowledge of construction, Aubrey's computer was his guide, and our friend Herbie also helped. Need I mention the wasted materials? But when completed everything looked as if done by skilled craftsmen. The mistake our visitors made was to compliment his work. They then had to endure scrutinising his achievements. Aubrey was like a boy with his new toys, every tool or machinery he needed for the job was purchased, he refused to rent anything.

I sometimes fretted over the expenditure, but most times smiled and indulged after seeing his elation of ownership. There were times when I was called upon to inspect every phase of the job. That I found tedious, he needed a more detail oriented wife. Our girls and their husbands were subjected to many hours of listening to all his plans for future projects. Since his passing, I'm sure sales have dropped at the hardware store.

Our lives as relocated expats were far from boring. We are blessed with siblings, lots of cousins in our age group whom we are close with and good friends. Victoria Day weekend was always our first big barbecue of the season and usually within a day or two of Aubrey's birthday. I always prepared his favourite food and the grands helped by blowing out the candles before he had the chance to make a wish. I bought him an ice cream maker and they all had fun using it. I believe those were Aubrey's best birthdays. How he adored and enjoyed our grandchildren. The last two summers prior to his passing he took us all to the CNE (Canadian National Exhibition) and although we packed coolers with healthy food, Aubrey insisted the kids eat all the junk food they desired. We enjoyed hotdogs, burgers, fries, ice cream and pop. He hung large bags of cotton candy from his belt and the kids went back and forth helping themselves. The coolers remained unopened on both occasions. Our grands went on the rides and played all day, much to their Grandy's delight. We all had a great time.

We were enjoying a comfortable routine lifestyle, nothing exciting, just peaceful, happy and fulfilling. We didn't travel anywhere, Aubrey claimed he'd had enough of travelling and didn't want to see another airport and I was content with his decision. He wasn't even interested in driving, I did most of it. As a matter of fact, the majority of wives returning to Canada did the driving whenever possible, simply because of the hair raising driving habits our husbands developed while living in the Kingdom. Ironically, Aubrey sometimes fretted about my chauffeuring skills and claimed I must have lead in my right foot. He also implied that growing older did not temper my impulsive behaviour. I had to agree with that statement, especially because of his umbrella incident.

We were on our way for our first annual medical check-up since returning and as usual, I was driving. I stopped at a T-junction at the traffic light where a man was pacing back and forth asking for money. Neither Aubrey nor I had any cash. I felt awful for not having any money for the guy. It started to rain as the light changed. I slowly moved forward and without a second thought, I grabbed the umbrella between our seats and threw it out to the man. Aubrey was silent until I completed the turn, then said, "You just threw my umbrella out the window!" I replied, "Yes, it's bad enough to resort to begging, doing so in the rain is pathetic. The poor man looked so sad, I hope I didn't hit him." Aubrey continued, sounding irritated, "Merle, that's the umbrella you bought me in London and tried justifying the outrageous price by showing me the carved mahogany handle and quality canopy. Now it's pouring, and we are close to the doctor's office!" I said, softly and calmly, for by then he was getting angry, and with just cause "Don't worry, I'll drop you off at the entrance." Aubrey snapped, "You know damn well I'm not going to agree to that!" My husband, always the gentleman, would usually be the one to go to the parking machine, pay and collect the receipt. I then thought, *"Merle, you did it this time! Why did you do such a stupid thing? And that man has no idea the quality of the umbrella thrown to him. Especially the beautifully carved handle, which was the main reason you bought it."* After what felt like an eternity of silence, while Aubrey was I'm sure, fuming silently, he abruptly said: "No one would believe this!" He looked at me angrily, then in a frustrated and resigned tone said, "Merle, what am I going to do with you? When the hell are you going to think before you act, and not let your heart motivate your actions?" I was wise enough to remain silent while we continued our journey. We both got wet that day. The following day I bought him another umbrella; not attractive, but functional and much cheaper. I still carry it around in my car.

On the fourth year after returning to Canada, it was time again for our annual medical check-up. Aubrey's blood work indicated some abnormalities. It took many months and numerous tests before the doctors' irrefutable evidence that my husband had leukaemia.

* * * * *

January 12/2016

My dear, dear Brey,

Today is a sad one for me. Everything regarding your illness seems to be the focus of my thoughts. Much to my sadness and regret, the months after you were diagnosed with leukaemia, were too short and hectic. Now reflecting, I would have liked to have spent every hour with you. One is never prepared for situations as such, and I'm sure regrets are common. When the oncologist Dr Ruimstein, in her best bedside manner, gave us the news, do you recall your first question to her? "How long do I have?" She then replied, "Twelve to eighteen months." I guess you heard me catch my breath, for you reached out, squeezed my hand saying calmly and quietly, "Don't cry!" I didn't. Your next words, to both the doctor's and my astonishment were, "Dr Ruimstein, this must be one of the toughest parts of your job; to deliver such news." The doctor was so awed by your statement, she reached out spontaneously and hugged you, saying, "Aubrey, in my entire career, no one has ever considered my thoughts or feelings, especially the patient. You are indeed a remarkable man!"

You must know Brey, during our years together, your calmness and tenacity in troubled times, always dissipated my fears and anxieties. You dealt with whatever stress and adversity with such incredible composure and style. With admiration, but deep sadness,

I watched you navigate your illness. You took each transition in stride and peppered the rough spots with wry humour; you always had a smile or words of appreciation for the doctors and nurses, even when discouraged and tired. Throughout your illness, in desperation I pleaded, 'Dear God please give me the strength, wisdom, and anything else needed, to comfort and help him.' In the early stages of your treatment, on a few occasions, you insisted we take the subway to your transfusion appointments. However, as you are aware, most times Tazra drove us, and between the three of us, especially Tazra, she never missed anything we discussed with the doctors. She retained all the information during those visits, and would patiently go over it all with me, especially when my emotions overrode the details. Other times Fermin accompanied us, he never hesitated and always arrived on time to get us to the hospital at 8am and spent the entire day with us. We returned home to your favourite meal prepared by Aliya when she did not accompany us to the hospital. She always cooked your favourite meals, especially the pasta, scallops and smoked salmon dish. I teased you about going for a blood transfusion only to get such a scrumptious meal. You also enjoyed the many curried lamb and roti dishes Areefa found the time – between her working hours – to prepare you.

Between the hospital visits, do you recall the many hours you spent in the garage working on something for our home? I think it was also your time to reflect and sort out your concerns. I joined you there a few times but I knew you preferred the solitude. Those were the moments I couldn't reach you, you seemed so reclusive and I could actually hear your thoughts, "Something inside of me is broken and I can't fix it!"

I made us countless cups of tea and you would then join me in the family room. It was on one such occasion that you said you didn't want your illness known to anyone. According to you, there was no physical discomfort as yet, and you could get on with living a normal life, without being reminded of your condition, by well-wishers. The girls and I respected your request. That was also when you suggested I speak with someone, maybe Khalda or Zorena, should I need to, but Aliya and Tazra were my confidants and they were sufficient. The girls and I found comfort in each other. I told my sisters of your illness, many months later. Incidentally, after you passed away, we got a few complaints from some relatives and friends as to why they were not informed about your illness. I appreciated where they were coming from, and explained that was your wish, and on no account was I going to violate your trust. I think they understood.

As you may recall, you and I had our moments of quietly talking, weeping, or just holding each other. One day while lying next to you chatting, remember you tried to explain again, what you thought I needed to know regarding our finances, the house, vehicles and other matters, which you considered important. This was nothing new, as you are aware, you always wanted me involved in our everyday affairs. I never bothered, knowing you would take care of everything. Feeling the warmth and comfort of lying next to you, and with the sad knowledge of how short lived this moment, I thought selfishly of myself. Sometime during your information and advice, I cried out, "I don't need to hear about all the mundane things. You and I shared such beautiful moments in the world, now please tell me how to continue appreciating and surviving without you!" You were silent after my outburst, as you squeezed me tightly against you. I later regretted my weakness. I didn't want you to worry about the girls and my survival after you were gone. I knew that bothered you sometimes.

Those were rough days for all of us, but especially you. How my heart broke for you. I prayed and sometimes felt angry with life. Looking back now, I should have been stronger and had more faith. God had blessed us. Though our years together seemed short, for He took you too early, but then anytime would have been too early. You went quickly and painlessly, for that I thank Him! I have to believe you are in a better place, and at peace with your soul.

Stay well, my darling!
My love always and beyond,
Your Nastyface

THIRTY

We lost Aubrey fourteen months after being diagnosed. He was a model patient and researched everything he could about leukaemia, which we all discussed in detail. He took the usual non-curing medicine, then refused the second experimental drug. Aubrey's rationale, it made him physically ill and he wanted the last months with us to be as lucid as possible. The girls and I tried to persuade him, but the final decision was his.

In the beginning he needed transfusions once a week. Then as time progressed, twice, until a week prior to his passing away, when no matter how many units of blood he received, it was futile. Because his immune system was very vulnerable, a common cold or fever could have taken him down. We avoided crowds and I refused invitations, always ready with an excuse.

Between doctors' appointments and blood transfusions, Aubrey went about doing the usual, mowing the lawn, working in the garage or in our home. As the months went by, everything became exceedingly difficult to accomplish but he refused help from our sons-in-law, insisting he was able, for now. I watched him struggling, and though my heart was breaking, I couldn't let him be anything but himself – independent, proud and determined.

The girls and I spent much time with him and when able, our sons-in-law joined us. Most times one of us accompanied him to the hardware store, then coffee or just us four hanging around discussing politics, especially American. We all agreed, had Aubrey been around during the Trump administration, he would have had a field day.

He and I also shared many precious moments together, mostly early in the mornings over cups of tea, chatting with our favourite music playing softly in the background. I always enjoyed Aubrey's company, advice, and mostly his humour. On those mornings, we never discussed his illness. I don't know if that was his or my decision. I never felt it was a wilful act of denial, we just always seemed to have a lot to talk and smile about. As Robertson Davies said, "*A great part of all the pleasure of love begins, continues and sometimes ends with conversation.*"

One day, he and Tazra went out, I had no idea where but somehow they ended up at a car dealership. Aubrey always loved cars, especially vintage ones. Later that day, Tazra told me about a white Mercedes he was admiring. Without a second thought and unknown to him, Tazra and I went and bought it. Yes, impetuous me, as usual. We looked over the vehicle with care, having no idea what to look for, then Tazra took it for a test drive. We were satisfied. Now to the bank. Adam our financial advisor, looked at me and asked, "Have you given this enough thought?" Before I could reply, Tazra said, "Please issue the bank draft, she's buying my dad the car." Adam knew about my husband's illness; Aubrey had invited him home to discuss our finances, explaining everything in detail for my benefit.

I bought the car, went home and arranged the insurance. Aliya and Tazra brought it home a couple of days later. That was one of the few times I recall surprising him. Throughout our years together, I rarely got the opportunity to do so. Whatever Aubrey wanted and could afford, he bought, leaving me with few choices or sometimes no choice, just a headache as to what to get him. In my frustration and desperation, I once went to a jeweller and had a couple pairs of silver collar stays made and engraved, simply because I knew every morning while dressing for work, he inserted them in his shirts.

A gift he also used and loved was a green malachite Montblanc pen set. Another time I gave him a recording of the girls, chatting and singing their hearts out. And in between all of the usual gifts of shirts, sweaters, cufflinks, leather and pens were a few lines from me, expressing my love and appreciation. Once while browsing through a little bookstore in Cambridge, England, I came across a huge old Bible and bought it mainly because I knew he would like the etchings. And of course, I was always researching reading material for him, first editions, old copies and limited publications.

Aubrey drove his car until he was too weak to continue. Chauffeuring then became my job again. I enjoyed the smooth ride, but found it too low; getting in and out was cumbersome. I sold it six months after he passed away.

* * * * *

March 4/2017

My darling Brey,

I think of you daily and often wondered in my own silly way, how could I have kept you alive, was there something I should have done, or not done? Then logical thoughts take over. After all, I am not God, nor a doctor, and my love was not sufficient to keep you with me.

I have all ninety-one letters you wrote me. I re-read and counted them through tears after you passed away. The first one in November 1965 and the last one incomplete and left on your computer, October 2014. The girls discovered it a few months after you passed away. Regretfully, I found only a few of my replies, I believe you placed the rest in the time capsule. Bet you never thought you wrote so many letters. Thank God you did, I find them most therapeutic and beautiful. Your sharp mind, wicked sense of humour, and always your great love. Reading your letters only reinforces, sharing life with you was a privilege and blessing.

Do you know, in our entire forty seven years together, I recall you telling me a few times that you loved me. I remember one particular incident vividly. You hugged me tightly from behind, and with deep emotion said, "God, how I love you!" Yet, your letters and actions convey it so beautifully. My darling, your crowning glory was the ability to express your love in so many ways, with no reservations, and not feel less of a man for doing so.

Life is lonely without you. Half of my heart is still with you, the other half struggling with the present. Like dealing with situations I have never previously encountered, both emotionally and physically. You have always shielded me from life's tribulations. Now I have to cope with some rough and stormy days. However, the next day, at most times, is better than the previous one. Brey, I know that I can't avoid some of the challenges of living alone but I can choose how to deal with them. I remember one of your many advices during our nightly chats in the hospital, "Merle, you have a good heart, follow it but don't have it trampled on." That statement was because of the conversation we had previously, when I claimed to like a few acquaintances. You asked if there was anyone I didn't like. You were serious, so I gave it some thought, and couldn't come up with a name. That was when you made me aware that I dislike no one I have ever encountered in life. Indifference, tolerance, but never dislike.

When sad or troubled thoughts keep me awake – which occurs most evenings – I have my talk with God, then listen to the music we both enjoyed. It does not hasten the process of falling asleep, it just makes it eventually more pleasant. Then there are times when I think of you with so much joy, I forget for a brief moment you are no longer with me. That's the wonder of loving you, thoughts of you and our life together, never fail to please my heart.

Since your passing, I think of death as another phase of mans' existence and have convinced myself into believing I'll be with you again. Perhaps I'm spiritual, living in a fantasy world or just plain crazy. But then, no one knows what really happens when our life on earth is over. Some believe we are buried and decomposed, or cremated and that's it, others think of reincarnation. Then there is always the controversy of Heaven and Hell. Since no proof is available and I am not religious enough to accept faithfully, I choose to believe I'll be with you again. And who could convince me otherwise? This may be a coward's way of preparing for the afterlife, but it certainly makes my life without you bearable and hopeful. When I feel sad, profoundly sad, that agonising empty feeling, beyond tears – which occurs most mornings just before dawn – I thank God for the privilege of having had you in my life. Our years together were not long enough, but the moments exceeded measure! Brey, you showed me the other side of everything and even beyond the stars! You read my mind, heard my heart and saw my soul."

My dearest, how I miss you! Especially now, this very moment! I hope you're behaving in heaven, I'm not there as yet to keep an eye on you. Heaven!! Do you recall, during one of our discussions about the existence or nonexistence of heaven, and hell? You claimed I'll go to Heaven and you Hell. Though boldly stating, you're definitely 'heavenly material.' However, when you get to the pearly gates, you'll ask, "Where is my wife being sent?" Of course, the Saint will say Heaven. You will then ask to be sent to Hell, for you would have had enough of me on earth.

Take care my love and remember, I'm always,
Your Merle

THIRTY-ONE

May 22/2016

Dear, dear Brey, (Yes, today on your birthday)

I think of your illness, with the little things, big things and everything unfolding. Two incidents must have hurt you. And I live with that remorse. One mid-morning, I brought you up a drink, and we chatted while you were having it. You then asked me to lay down beside you. I fully intended to but had to attend to some soup on the stove, which took only a few minutes. I must have gotten distracted because I forgot to return. When I remembered and returned, you were asleep and the moment when you needed me had passed. How I regret that, you never requested much and when you did, I failed you. Please forgive me. The other time, I was invited to Anissa's baby shower. I had no intentions of going, for my heart and head were too occupied with you. As you know, I refused all invitations to gatherings, I couldn't risk contracting anything, a common cold would have been disastrous for you. On this occasion the girls and you insisted I go. I guess you thought the outing was worth the risk. I went reluctantly. After a few glasses of some concoction Yvonne kept pouring me, I felt relaxed and was actually enjoying the company. No one knew of your illness, so it was not a topic I had to discuss, or answer any questions about. At one point I felt I should call home but that was getting back to reality, the constant sadness, worry, but more so, that helpless feeling. As you know, throughout our years together, we always phoned each other at some point when we were apart. I failed to do so this time. When I returned home, do you remember saying quietly, more resignedly than accusingly, "You didn't call." I replied honestly, "I didn't feel up to it". You were silent. I immediately regretted my answer and felt like curling up in a corner, totally disgusted with myself. I should have fabricated some excuse but my love, you would have seen through that, and we respected each other too much to lie. How my heart hurt for you that evening. I went for a shower, my weeping place at home. Later, Tazra and Aliya tried to make me feel better by saying, I needed the break much more than I thought. That didn't ease my conscience or heart. I constantly remember those two incidents with much sadness and regret. And just wanted you to know how sorry, so deeply sorry I am. Forgive me.

I'm sure you'll hear from me again tomorrow morning. Take care dearest.

My love always and beyond,
Merle

* * * * *

December 18/2016

My Brey,

If there was anything meaningful or positive about your illness, it was the week you and I spent time in the hospital in palliative care. I remember everything we discussed when the lights were out. How we revealed our innermost thoughts. They were happy, funny, loving and occasionally sad. We did not hold back. I think you and

I had finally come to terms with the fact that our time together was limited and we made the most of every waking hour. And boy, were you chatty! I always thought that was my role in our marriage. I guess you were determined to have the last say. My darling, I will always treasure those nights, the many times I heard your heart and saw your soul. Some thoughts we shared, so sacred, will remain locked in my heart, never to be revealed. We talked for hours. Apart from advising what car I should buy and explaining again, in detail about our investments, you also recalled so many little insignificant incidents that after they occurred, I never gave them another thought but you remembered! Even with all the medication, your memory was as sharp as prior to your illness. As you once said, "this sickness will destroy my body, but not my brain!"

For instance, you talked about some uneventful moments. Like, while you were a student, I sometimes prepared you a steak dinner. This rarely occurred and only when you went to the library and came home late, hence, you ate alone. Knowing you would never want a steak, unless I was also having one, you sometimes asked what I had for dinner, I always replied, "same as you". Now after so many years, you related to me in the hospital, you knew I never did have any steak. Our budget didn't allow it. You just indulged my fibs.

One night, you were restless, remember I got out of my bed and sat at the foot of yours and massaged your feet while we chatted. I just wanted to distract you from any negative thoughts. That was when I thanked you for loving me so much. What I really wanted to do, was to lay beside you and hold you close to me, but by then you were weak and frail, I was scared of hurting you. Remember, I joked about how hospitals should have double beds. I also recall telling you that particular night, how I loved your soul, your unconditional love, your laughter and even when I looked my worst, how you still reached for me. I wonder if you ever realised how beautiful and comforting that feeling was.

Another evening, while chatting randomly about whatever came to mind, I asked how come during your student days you never fretted over my spending one fifth of our grocery money on flowers, when we could barely afford the necessities. You replied, "I used to watch you clip the stems and change the water so often, trying to preserve them a little longer, how could I have objected to the pleasure you derived from them? Life is not about food alone". We also talked about your youthful days in Guyana and all the funny incidents, especially with your "drunken friends", as you referred to them.

But the most poignant of all our nightly chats was the time we were discussing your medication. You know exactly what I mean!! That was the evening, when you said, "Let's not talk about my illness or those damn tablets. I want to talk about us". After a few seconds of silence, you sounded as if in deep thought and speaking to yourself. You said "You know, I can't ever remember not loving you, it seems as if I've loved you all my life." That statement was said softly, sincerely and tenderly, so unlike your usual teasing tone. I was lost for words. Replying, "I love you too," would have sounded inadequate. My tears flowed as I buried my face in my pillow trying to be silent. You then asked if I was asleep. The lump in my throat made speech difficult. I tried to control my emotion and answered in a choked voice. "No my love, I heard you!" Our conversation ceased after that, both knowing the other was awake but with such full hearts, words were not necessary. I laid awake until I knew you were asleep, then quietly got out of bed, paced the corridor and had my nightly moments of thoughts and tears. While walking round and round the corridor, I sobbed uncontrollably that particular evening. The nurses at the station supplied me with tissues every night as I passed them, that evening I was handed a warm, moist towel. Those kind nurses, God bless them all!

You know Brey, this business of love is so complex. It tears you apart when denied, but when fulfilled, your heart soars beyond the heavens. God's masterpiece, in my opinion, was when he gave man the ability to feel for each other; to want to climb into your mate's soul and remove any hurt or pain; to pretend all is well, just to see relief on your love's face; to trust unconditionally; to respect with dignity; and most of all, to love beyond time. That evening was one of the moments I asked God to take me with you. I didn't even think of our girls, and how selfish my request was at that particular moment. You seemed so helpless and vulnerable, so unlike my Brey. I just wanted to love and protect you, and whatever else it took to make you well and happy. Writing all of this is making me too sad. I'll change the mood.

Remember our battles at home over the baby monitor? You weren't quite so weak but I still wanted to be upstairs whenever you got out of bed. You constantly turned your monitor off, trying not to be a bother; I in the meantime, had mine on and listened while I did my chores. Thinking you were asleep, I would suddenly hear you moving about and not from the monitor but from the squeaking floor. Your platelets were low most days. Falling and cutting yourself could have led to serious haemorrhaging. Stubborn as usual, you were. Those were trying times, with you, me and the baby monitor. I recall you once told me to leave you alone. You sounded so harsh, my eyes filled with tears. I left the room and ran downstairs. Tazra heard you and hugged me saying, "Dad shouldn't speak to you in that tone of voice". I immediately pulled away, claiming I'll take whatever you dish out. After all, I'm not the one dying and can't imagine the frustration, anger, fear and any other emotion you were going through. One day while applying lotion on your body, remember you said, "Merle, I don't *mind dying, after all it's inevitable, it's the business of it. And I hate putting you through all this business."*

Brey, I say with all sincerity, during your illness, I never once felt tired or you were too much of a bother or work. Loving you so much erased all of those feelings.

My darling, I have convinced myself into believing death didn't really part us. For me this is just a heart wrenching, temporary separation. Dear God, I pray my conviction is right!

I must stop now, my love. Will write again soon. In the meantime, enjoy wherever you are, but no women. I don't care where you are, heaven, hell or elsewhere, NO WOMEN!!

*My love always and beyond,
Merle*

THIRTY-TWO

Aubrey wanted to spend his last days at home with us. I promised when he was ready, I would do what was necessary to get him there. The doctors felt he was too weak and didn't recommend the move but my determined husband proved them wrong. He requested a walker and paced the corridor, convincing the doctors he still had some strength left.

He was released and sent home in an ambulance accompanied by Aliya. I followed in my car, for reasons unknown, I didn't want this mode of transportation with him. The girls, grandchildren and I kept him as comfortable and entertained as possible. Our grands decorated our bedroom walls with their art and we played his favourite music. Aliya or I sometimes read to him. Tazra sorted and dispensed the oxygen when necessary. We were also busy containing the flow of blood from his nostrils and throat while trying not to look anxious, or fuss over him. He disliked too much attention.

There was little opportunity to contemplate on how much longer Aubrey would be with us. Every moment with him was busy and precious. He didn't have much of an appetite and his last meal – at his request, which was the day prior to his passing and at approximately 10 am – was sour cream and onion potato chips and a Heineken beer.

On the fourth day after being released from the hospital, Aubrey passed away. His doctor came to make the transition as comfortable as possible, and we also had a nurse in attendance. Tazra, Aliya and I never left his side. As Aubrey's time with us drew nearer, he became a little restless, I remember whispering in his ear "Go to sleep, my love." It took all the willpower I could muster, not to weep. He once told me, when the time came, he didn't want his last sight of us, crying.

My husband closed his eyes and seemed asleep, although I knew his heart had stopped beating. I will never forget, part of me went with Aubrey that day and part of him will always be here with me. Now, reflecting with deep sadness but much pride, my guy approached his death as he lived his life. With grace and dignity! It took me a while to condition my brain and mostly my heart, to accept the fact that my love was elsewhere and there will be a void in my life.

Days later, I saw my dressing gown in the laundry basket, the front covered with Aubrey's blood. Not recalling how this occurred, I asked the girls. They said after he passed away I embraced him, his face against my stomach, crying uncontrollably, I don't recall that. What I do remember was being able to sleep throughout the first night, awaking with the thought, "This is most surprising, Aubrey is gone and I slept through the night." That night made up for all the sleepless ones. I was exhausted both emotionally and physically. Also, I guess the thought that he had passed away, had not fully sunk in.

On the first anniversary of his death, I woke before dawn as usual, reached for my iPad, wrote and sent the following to our relatives and friends.

* * * * *

October 29/2015

Dear All,

Today the 29th is a year since I've lost Aubrey. My heart is ever so sad, I remember everything, more so the last two weeks of his life. Especially the week we spent in the hospital together. How I fed him, and held him close to me. One shower I particularly recall. He sat on the shower chair, we had fun horsing around, or rather I did. My love looked at me tenderly, laughed a little, and I felt good! When the nurse came in and saw water everywhere, the floor, walls and I fully clothed but drenched, she smiled and mopped up. The toughest part of that week was not letting him see me cry. For this whole business was not about me, only Aubrey and how to help him find peace within himself and die with dignity. Hope I succeeded!

Aubrey's last four days at home with us were devastating. There was no time to sleep, cry or think. Between the girls and I, we never left his side. I never loved or felt prouder of Aliya and Tazra as I did when I saw the way they took care of their father, with such tenderness, patience and love. I also have to give much credit to my sons-in-law Reagan and Braden for their support, cooking and caring for the grands while leaving the girls free to do as they see fit. I am blessed with the family I have.

My life with Aubrey was complete with love, laughter, arguments, passion, loyalty and always admiration. He was totally unique in my eyes and maybe that's how it should be between lovers. I miss our friendship, chats over a cup of tea and yes, even our fights, which I provoked most times. He would say, "Merle, no one aggravates me like you!" I always replied. "And you love no one, like you do me". My replies didn't always go over well, it all depended on the level of his anger.

I started out feeling sad and alone, I am now much better, after all, I loved and was loved from October *1961* to October *2014*. How more blessed can one be? I will always miss Aubrey but I also know my life must move on, I have the girls and their families to consider.

I thank all of you for listening patiently while I talked endlessly about Aubrey. You can't imagine the comfort I derived in doing so ... And you listened!

The girls and their families will be here today, my grands are always a beautiful distraction.

Much gratitude and love for your committed support.
Merle

* * * * *

November 21/2019

My darling Brey,

I see better through the tears. Time is indeed a blessing, it soothes, comforts and heals the heart. It is now 2:16am, I suddenly woke up and have the urge to say something. Anything to you! So, I will just write whatever comes to mind.
 How I love you, please don't be too tired of hearing me say so, I need to. You were so much a part of me, my strength and light. I grew up in your arms, trusted you implicitly, laughed, cried and was at peace with my soul. How blessed we were, now I must not be sad. You are no longer here physically but all that we lived through is still alive and vibrant and they comfort me. If there was more to life, I didn't miss it or cared. God had chosen us to be together and that was sufficient.
 And what a couple Brey! Throughout our years together, you always had the will and determination to make things happen, whereas, I depended mostly on faith and hope, especially when my neglectful attitude kept getting in the way! With the blessing came some wicked arguments, remember those moments? I always regarded our disagreements as trivial matters. Yes, trivial to me, you took life more seriously. I guess one of us had to be that way, if not we surely would not have survived with my attitude.
 As you are aware, I prioritise when dealing with my misfortunes, battles, disappointments etc. in life. And

quoting you "Merle, I see you assessing the situation, and if you feel it wouldn't kill you, you ignore it." Touché! I know, bad attitude. You picked up the slack most times over what I regarded as 'temporary inconveniences', like appointments, money and all the mundane things involved with everyday living. But anything regarding the health and happiness of you and our girls were always my priority. And I did what was necessary, regardless, to keep you three well and happy. That's where my strength and loyalty lie. And why, I presume, you didn't get too flustered when I forgot, neglected, or ignored what I considered the trivialities. Because you knew, I would relocate the earth for you and our girls. The only confusion was how I went about doing it!

Aliya and Tazra still discuss their concerns or problems with me. They know that's when I cease being their mother and try to help by assessing the situation as logically, equitably and morally possible. Then silly me, when they are not around, I sometimes weep for not having you to support my advice. I remember, one day you and I were having a heated discussion, or rather argument. I forgot to send a cheque to a contractor and something else which I don't recall at the moment, except because of my neglect, it cost us much more, financially. You were so angry! Fretting about how you can't depend on me to carry out a simple task. I have to agree with you, my appalling ways did astound even me, at times! Of course, though at fault, I was defensive. Humility is a virtue I must practice more. There were times when I should have admitted my fault and maintained some sort of decorum. However, this was not that moment. Do you remember I said, "You should have married someone like Mary. Boring, no opinion, quiet, agrees with everything you say and a good housekeeper. Oh! And she'll remember to mail the damn cheque, which you should have done yourself!" Your reply was, "Anything right now to bring more order in my life and less of your *mouth!" Ouch! That did hurt. I remembered the incident long enough to bring it up later, and asked if you would have preferred a docile partner. One who would be your housekeeper, secretary, confidant, lover and psychologist. In other words, a robot. You hugged me saying, "Food for thought! Imagine, to live with no hypertension, frustration, headaches and aggravation. Though, to go through life without those vices, is not having you. That I can't imagine or want, but Merle, you do try my faith sometimes! I just continue to hope for improvement." And my darling I was tempted, but refrained from saying, "When pigs fly! That's the time I will curb my tongue and be more organised". Having said that, do you recall the many times I succumbed during some of our arguments? It took me many years to learn, why and when, my pride should take a back seat.*

Seriously Brey, there must be some logic to 'opposites attract'. We were different in some ways. And boy, did those 'ways' cause some anger. But all through the disagreements, I knew our love for each other was never compromised. That was steadfast and after an hour or two, we were friends/lovers again. Who knows? Maybe I instigated those rows because the reconciliation was so delicious. Now you will never know, my love. That! You will never know! I can actually hear you thinking, "I thought dying would have spared me her chatter". I will stop, my iPad needs charging. Yes, the same one you gave me with the card, "I hope you learn to use this before I die". I did many months later.

*So long Breybrey,
My love always and beyond,
Merle*

THIRTY-THREE

This letter was written on an especially rough morning after Aubrey passed away.

* * * * *

Nov. 26/2016

My Brey,

This morning I stood gazing at your photograph on the refrigerator door and started to cry. Since you've been gone it takes so little to reduce me to tears. The photograph I refer to is the one with you walking on the sand dunes, away from the camera. I think Tazra took that, unknown to you, when they came in on holiday, while in university. Sand dunes! And I think sacrosanct. That picture reminds me of the Arab proverb "The further man walks into the desert, the closer he gets to God." You knew how much I loved the desert but did you ever know how moved, beyond words, I felt every time I was there? Talking, even whispering, seemed an intrusion. There was that feeling of serenity, silence and wonder in the dunes. A place where I always felt the need to thank God for being alive. If ever I felt spiritual it was there, especially at sunrise, when dawn reached the horizon; my breath was caught, then suddenly, taken away in a glance. The rippling sand looked like a riverbed when the tide was out. Clean, loose red sand, one could easily be lost in its vastness and beauty. Knowing my passion for the desert, Tahay sent me this excerpt from 'The Road to Mecca' by Muhammad Assad.

"There are many more beautiful landscapes in the world but none, I think, that can shape man's spirit in so sovereign a way. The desert is bare and clean and knows no compromise. It sweeps out of the heart of man all the lovely fantasies that could be used as a masquerade for wishful thinking, and thus makes him free to surrender himself to an Absolute that has no image: the farthest of all that is far and yet the nearest of all that is near."

Thank you my love, for taking me to the desert when possible. I knew for you it was just another interesting part of the world. For me, the closest to heaven! Do you recall, for my fortieth birthday, you arranged a scrumptious breakfast in the dunes? You bought my favourite food from the French Corner. And on that cool February morning I broke bread with you, the girls and the Jhangiani family. After breakfast I was left alone to wander about for a while, you always referred to my wanderings as, bonding with my God. For me it was a perfect way to start any day.

Remember when we returned home your boss called inviting us over for dinner. I would have preferred to end the day quietly with you and the girls. Apart from that, half a day in the desert zaps one's energy. You consoled me with, "just a short visit, we'll leave as soon as possible." As we dressed, you suggested I change into another outfit. This was not unusual; my mode of attire was never up to your standards. You always thought I underdressed and sometimes fretted about buying me such lovely jewellery when I hardly wear them. I changed my outfit and adorned myself with a few pieces of jewellery. Always the impeccable dresser, Mater once told me the story about you at four. A button was missing from your shirt and you refused to leave the bedroom. That irritated her but your nanny came to the rescue and pleaded for you, Mater sewed on the button. The only time I've ever seen you a little less groomed, was when I came out of the operating room after Tazra's birth. You looked so stressed. Coping with Aliya, school and finances, was taking its toll. My heart broke for you. The nurse thought they were tears of jubilation, you knew differently, because when I reached out and touched your shirt, you whispered, "My jacket covered the wrinkles." After you passed away, I sent a photograph of you to Ken, he referred to you as, "The debonair Mr Miller". I thought it was the most appropriate description.

Now back to my birthday story. On our way to your boss's villa we paused to chat with Antoine, who was watering their garden. After wishing me a happy birthday again, he invited us in for a quick drink. The previous evening, as you may recall, we had a pre birthday dinner with them and did the usual cake and gifts. At the entrance, Anastasia greeted us with hugs, and as I walked into the living room shouts of "surprise" from about twenty of our friends; expats from Turkey, England, India, Jamaica, Cyprus, Lebanon, Greece, Jordan, and Canada. We ate, talked, laughed and danced away the remaining hours of my special day. Our dear and thoughtful friend Anastasia, arranged my surprise party and didn't even tell you until after we returned from the desert. I thought it strange that your boss called so late inviting us to dinner but then entertaining in Saudi Arabia was most times impromptu.

I'm sure you recall the years we shared; I just like reliving them with you. I seem to have so much time to remember. I know you're thinking "I still can't shut her up". I'll go now but you'll hear from me again. Sooner than you think!

My love always and beyond,
Merle

* * * * *

August 13/2017

Hello there Breybrey,

While at the supermarket yesterday, I heard a mother calling her son "Teddy" and instantly thought of the girls' pet hamsters Bruno and Teddy. January 1, 1983. Do you recall that far back? Yes, on Aliya's birthday, Bruno passed away. And Aliya's distressed voice saying to you, "And on my birthday Dad, on my birthday!" You wrapped him in one of your best white silk handkerchiefs and buried him in the backyard. Bruno was a popular guy, quite a few of the neighbourhood kids were in attendance.

    Aliya's favourite food prepared for her birthday was left uneaten. You and I felt guilty for not having lost our appetite. Remember, I suggested we sit in front of the television with our plates on our laps, rather than on the well-set birthday table. We had to display some sort of empathy, for our girls were totally distraught. It was a day of mourning in the Miller household! Teddy kept the wheel rolling. I don't recall when he joined Bruno in the animal heaven.

    While on the subject of animals, I remembered how you indulged the kids and I regarding the menagerie of stray cats I fed daily, some looked like Siamese, Savannah, Persian, etc. The high walls around our compound never phased the cats scaling them. Their scarred, mangy and hungry looks won me over, so I started putting out food for them. You fretted at first, eventually giving up. I bought some paediatric antibiotics, banana flavour, while thinking, "what's good for babies, hopefully will be alright for cats." As you are aware, one could buy any antibiotic over the counter, I started to add it to their food. You were impressed as to how well they improved. Remember the names I gave them? Scarface, Mangy, Snots, Greedy, Red Eyes, Limpy, etc. All descriptive and by no means sentimental.

During an extensive period, we were feeding seven stray cats twice a day. They came, ate and then disappeared over the walls until the next mealtime. Do you recall the Friday I ran out of cat food and you were reluctant to take me to the supermarket? That was all I needed, anyhow you relented and off we went. I placed a dozen cans of food in our cart, you then emptied the shelf – all twenty-three more cans. I counted them when we got home – I guess you didn't want to be bothered for a while. At the checkout I moved ahead, because of prayer call they started to close. I heard the cashier say in a friendly voice, "You've got cats!" I also heard your answer, "No, I don't". The dear man shifted uncomfortably and was silent throughout the transaction. I was at the supermarket's entrance and not close enough to explain.

On our way home, I asked, "Why didn't you tell the cashier we were feeding stray cats?" Remember your reply? "He asked if I had cats, well I don't, what else was there to say?" That was typical of you my love, never the small talk man. The cashier must have thought, "Thank God, I'll never be invited to their home for supper!"

I knew you cared for animals, those strays proved me right. I observed how you looked at them amusingly through the patio door while they ate. You were just not in the mood that Friday for cat food shopping. My *darling, you were full of compassion for the less fortunate and animals. All in all, a true underdog fighter. I loved that in you!*

Stay well in your corner of heaven. The girls and I are ok.

My love always and beyond,
Merle

THIRTY-FOUR

Now, years later, there is so much to laugh about, and sometimes, cry a little. My waking hours are not sufficient to indulge in all the memories. My life was interesting with Aubrey in it. There was always something to laugh at, to ponder and to learn. He had a great capacity to make any anecdote interesting or funny.

Throughout our years together, I enjoyed our debates, even our arguments, many times he got so riled up, I had to curb my smile.

When all is said and done, memories of my life with Aubrey keep interrupting my day-to-day existence. Oh, but what beautiful memories to sustain me!

Unknown to the girls and I, Aubrey had written a farewell letter to me. I cannot explain my thoughts or feelings when Aliya discovered it by accident on his computer. It was a few months after he passed away, when the girls and I were still emotionally distraught.

While reading Aubrey's letter I experienced elation, shock, reverence and surprise, but more so, deep sadness. Regretfully, because of time, emotion or lack of energy, he did not complete it.

* * * * *

October 2014

Farewell my dearest Merle. I am glad to have this opportunity to share with you a few things I should have done before. But as you know, we get involved with life and make the assumption that time is on our side and we will always be able to say the things we have in our heart. Some depart this world without having the opportunity to let their loved ones know how they really feel, or to apologise for any wrong or hurt they may have inflicted on their spouse. I am grateful my sickness gave me the opportunity to reflect on my life and relationship with you and my family.

My dearest, dearest Merle, first of all I would like to let you know, I have loved you from the very first time I met you and that love has endured to the end. Surprisingly, I never thought it would end like this. I had always hoped we would go together, or I would be the last to go. But like most things in life, it was not our decision to make. My life has been a happy, long and wonderful trip. Full of joy and remarkable moments.

I am sure there were times when I have been difficult to live with. For that, I am truly sorry. Please forgive my impatience, please forgive me for wanting everything to be perfect, please forgive my spontaneous outburst of anger. I may have said many other things which I cannot remember but nonetheless they must have really hurt you. For those incidents, I am terribly sorry and if possible, I would go back in time and erase them.

Please look over our grandchildren and help them to grow with strong values, integrity, honesty and pride in anything they do.

And thank you my darling for a wonderful life, the care and love, especially during my sickness. It was tough leaving, not because I fear what is beyond, I was just not ready to leave. Our life together was just a period in your life. Do not waste the remaining days you have left mourning for me. Go ahead and enjoy yourself.

* * * * *

April 3/2020

Dear Lily, Ruby, Jasper and Leo

Today is five years, five months and five days since your Grandy passed away. Also, it would have been our 53rd wedding anniversary. I am at a good place emotionally and a great part of that is because of your constant presence in my life. My heart glows with pride and love for you four.

Your Grandy was looking forward to growing up with you. He wanted to show you all the beauty and mystery around and beyond. And couldn't wait to assist with your mathematical problems; sit under the stars and talk about Galileo and the galaxies; or the doctrine of many other great men and women who have influenced our way of thinking. And also share some of his childhood memories. I cannot compare with his wisdom or analytical mind but I know he would approve of my bits of advice for you to try to live by.

My dearest favourite four, regardless of how downtrodden you may feel, believe in a higher being – much comfort, strength and faith is derived in doing so.

Respect and appreciate everyone's religion and beliefs; they also have the right to think and choose as they please.

Let empathy be a part of your daily life.

(Left to right) Lily, Leo, Jasper and Ruby, Canadian National Exhibition, 2013

When confronted with difficult situations, think positively; negativity stains the soul, and remember, few things in life are detrimental.

Whatever kindness you may extend to anyone, let it be known only from your heart to God's approval.

Always look for the good in change and try to adapt.

Avoid confrontations; temper hinders logic and wisdom.

Pursue your passion and dreams, but never at anyone's expense.

Understand and appreciate your past, look forward to the future but stay focused and live in the present.

I hope you choose your battles wisely, for you will be confronted with some; but when so, have the courage to voice your thoughts and the wisdom to listen and observe silently.

A favourite quote of mine is by Elizabeth Bibesco: "Give without remembering and take without forgetting."

Be thoughtful, loving and respectful to your Mom and Dad; their love for you is enduring, you will experience this wonder only when you, yourselves, are parents.

Most importantly, love with no restraints, it brings pure joy! Sustaining a meaningful relationship is a long journey but worth every step. One day, when you bond with your soulmate, wrapped around your heart should also be kindness, forgiveness and tolerance.

And, lastly, remember to keep your eyes on rainbows as you pray, dream and make things happen.

May you forever be in God's favour.

My love always,
Grammie

ACKNOWLEDGEMENTS

My heartfelt thanks to Kash Ali of Hansib Publications for regarding this project as a labour of love. Also, for tolerating my relentless emails and phone calls, all the while assuring me that I will get exactly what I want. And, dear nephew, you delivered! Mairi Norris and Chris Norris, and Helen Pompilio, I thank you for the time spent on your light-touch edits while retaining my own voice. Serena Jhangiani of The Vellum Group, LLC, many thanks for your expertise on the cover. Shamie Daligadu and Ronald Daligadu, I appreciate your help during the early stages of this book. Knowing I was not computer savvy, you exercised the patience of Job while speaking technical jargon to me. And Shimmy, thanks for transcribing Aubrey's letters. Kenneth Jarvis, many thanks for your constant encouragement to, "Move on; find a cause; a passion; write a book!" But more so, Ken, for your friendship. Tahay Balkissoon, my spiritual friend, you always insisted I write as my heart dictates. For that advice, I thank you! Yvonne Naraine, for my endless phone calls, regardless of time, and your soothing, "I know, Baab." And Lily Eve Aubrey Smith, my little computer guru. I thank you for your kindness and patience when sorting photographs and getting me out of endless computer mishaps. My brother, Arif Ali, for your unwavering support, wisdom and love. And the many other relatives and friends too numerous to mention, but whom I have the privilege to laugh with; to cry with; and to love unconditionally. I will always remember your kindness which I could never repay. You know who you are and I thank you!

And forever, Aliya Miller and Tazra Miller, my beacons throughout, for your commitment to putting my happiness first. You filled many desolate days with your love and thoughtfulness, even though your hearts were also hurting ... I See You!!